HARPER LEE'S

To Kill A Mockingbird

BY

Joyce Milton

SERIES EDITOR

Michael Spring
Editor, *Literary Cavalcade*
Scholastic Inc.

Room 412

BARRON'S EDUCATIONAL SERIES, INC.
Woodbury, New York / London / Toronto / Sydney

ACKNOWLEDGMENTS

We would like to acknowledge the many painstaking hours of work Holly Hughes and Thomas F. Hirsch have devoted to making the *Book Notes* series a success.

© Copyright 1984 by Barron's Educational Series, Inc.

All inquiries should be addressed to:
Barron's Educational Series, Inc.
113 Crossways Park Drive
Woodbury, New York 11797

Library of Congress Catalog Card No. 84-18431

International Standard Book No. 0-8120-3446-5

Library of Congress Cataloging in Publication Data
Milton, Joyce.
    Harper Lee's To kill a mockingbird.

    (Barron's book notes)
    Summary: A guide to reading "To Kill A Mockingbird"
with a critical and appreciative mind. Includes
background on the author's life and times, sample tests, term
paper suggestions, and a reading list.
    1. Lee, Harper. To kill a mockingbird. [1. Lee,
Harper. To kill a mockingbird. 2. American literature
—History and criticism] I. Title.
PS3562.E353T635   1984   813'.54   84-18431
    ISBN 0-8120-3446-5 (pbk.)

CONTENTS

ADVISORY BOARD

HOW TO USE THIS BOOK

You have to know how to approach literature in order to get the most out of it. This *Barron's Book Notes* volume follows a plan based on methods used by some of the best students to read a work of literature.

Begin with the guide's section on the author's life and times. As you read, try to form a clear picture of the author's personality, circumstances, and motives for writing the work. This background usually will make it easier for you to hear the author's tone of voice, and follow where the author is heading.

Then go over the rest of the introductory material—such sections as those on the plot, characters, setting, themes, and style of the work. Underline, or write down in your notebook, particular things to watch for, such as contrasts between characters and repeated literary devices. At this point, you may want to develop a system of symbols to use in marking your text as you read. (Of course, you should only mark up a book you own, not one that belongs to another person or a school.) Perhaps you will want to use a different letter for each character's name, a different number for each major theme of the book, a different color for each important symbol or literary device. Be prepared to mark up the pages of your book as you read. Put your marks in the margins so you can find them again easily.

Now comes the moment you've been waiting for—the time to start reading the work of literature. You may want to put aside your *Barron's Book Notes* volume until you've read the work all the way through. Or you may want to alternate, reading the *Book Notes* analysis of each section as soon as you have finished reading the corresponding part of the original. Before you move on, reread crucial passages you don't fully understand. (Don't take this guide's analysis for granted—make up your own mind as to what the work means.)

Once you've finished the whole work of literature, you may want to review it right away, so you can firm up your ideas about what it means. You may want to leaf through the book concentrating on passages you marked in reference to one character or one theme. This is also a good time to reread the *Book Notes* introductory material, which pulls together insights on specific topics.

When it comes time to prepare for a test or to write a paper, you'll already have formed ideas about the work. You'll be able to go back through it, refreshing your memory as to the author's exact words and perspective, so that you can support your opinions with evidence drawn straight from the work. Patterns will emerge, and ideas will fall into place; your essay question or term paper will almost write itself. Give yourself a dry run with one of the sample tests in the guide. These tests present both multiple-choice and essay questions. An accompanying section gives answers to the multiple-choice questions as well as suggestions for writing the essays. If you have to select a term paper topic, you may choose one from the list of suggestions in this book. This guide also provides you with a reading list, to help you when you start research for a term paper, and a selection of provocative comments by critics, to spark your thinking before you write.

THE AUTHOR AND HER TIMES

When *To Kill A Mockingbird* was first published in 1960, interviewers who met the author often felt as if they were coming face to face with a grownup version of Scout Finch, the six-year-old heroine of the novel. Although she was almost thirty-five years old, Harper Lee was a youthful looking woman with angular features and a casual, short-cropped hairstyle that marked her as a former tomboy.

Appearances were not deceiving. A brief glance at the facts of Lee's life shows that reviewers were right to suspect that the portrait of Scout was to a large degree autobiographical. Harper Lee grew up in the deep South in Monroeville, Alabama, a place very much like the imaginary town of Maycomb described in the novel. She was born in 1926, which would make her roughly the same age as Scout in the mid-1930s when the novel takes place. Like Atticus Finch in the story, Miss Lee's father Amasa C. Lee was a small-town lawyer with an unusual first name. The Lee family was descended from the famous Confederate Civil War general Robert E. Lee, and so—like the Finches in the novel—had every reason to take pride in its ancestry. Finally, Lee's mother's maiden name was Frances Finch.

As a child Lee was called by her first name, Nelle, a name she dropped in her adult years. She was only seven years old when she decided she wanted to become a writer, but it was many years before her dream was fulfilled. In the meantime Miss Lee studied law, following in the footsteps of her father and older sister. She attended the University of Alabama, and spent a year in England as an exchange student at Oxford University.

In 1950 Lee left the university without completing the requirements for a law degree. She moved to New York City where she worked as an airlines reservation clerk. Her childhood desire to become a writer now returned and she spent evenings and spare time working on essays and short stories. Eventually she got up the courage to show a few of her best pieces to a New York literary agent. The agent liked one of the stories and suggested that it be expanded into a novel.

On the basis of this encouragement, Lee decided to quit her airlines job and devote herself full time to writing. The decision meant she would have to sacrifice some comforts. She moved into a shabby apartment that did not even have hot water. She made do with whatever furniture she could pick up free or construct from orange crates and other discards. She was not able to work without interruption, however. Just as she was making some progress on her novel, her father suffered a sudden illness. From then on she made extended visits back home, dividing her time between New York and Alabama.

It turned out that the trips to Alabama were not a bad thing as far as her novel was concerned. Being home again brought Lee closer to the scene of her childhood memories of her relationship with her father, and the time she had spent with him at the courthouse. There was even an old house in her neighborhood where it had been rumored that the owner was a mysterious recluse, rather like the Boo Radley character in *To Kill A Mockingbird*.

While much of the background for the novel came from Lee's childhood experiences, the plot was primarily drawn from her imagination. As a result of her study of law, Lee was familiar with numerous cases involving a black man convicted on the basis of little or no solid evidence of raping a white woman. These incidents were transformed by the author into the fictional case of Tom Robinson that makes up the central portion of the novel. Lee later told an interviewer that she never thought of her years studying law as wasted effort, since she was forced to develop her skills in logical thinking and clear writing. Also, legal cases provided her with a fertile source of story ideas.

It was 1957 before Lee managed to finish a draft of her novel. The first editor who read the manuscript turned it down, explaining that it was nothing more than a series of short stories strung together. Lee agreed with the criticism, and took the draft back for reworking. With help from her editor, Lee spent the next two and a half years transforming the manuscript into the novel you know today as *To Kill A Mockingbird*. There were many times when she became discouraged and doubted that the book would ever be published. She later said that these years remained in her memory as "a long and hopeless period of writing the book over and over again."

Finally in 1960 *To Kill A Mockingbird* was ready for publication. The reception of the novel made up for all the years of hard work and struggle. Not only was the book well liked by reviewers, it was an instant success with readers young and old. Several book clubs, including the Literary Guild, chose the novel as a selection. The movie rights were sold almost immediately, the story becoming the basis for a successful movie starring Gregory Peck in the role of the small-town lawyer Atticus Finch. In 1961 Lee's success was crowned with a Pulitzer Prize for fiction, making her the first woman to win the award since 1942.

As a result of the success of her first novel, Harper Lee became something of a celebrity. She was the subject of articles in such magazines as *Life* and *Newsweek,* and the elite fashion magazine *Vogue* published one of her essays. It soon became apparent that Lee did not enjoy being the center of so much attention. Although by no means a hermit, she seemed to have some of the impulse that led people like her eccentric character Boo Radley to avoid public exposure. Lee insisted that in spite of her success she still considered herself a journeyman writer, and she turned aside attempts to get her to answer personal questions with witty but not very revealing answers. Having returned to Alabama to work on her second novel, Lee complained that even there it was difficult to find the privacy she needed to work without interruption. In the South, she said, friends and neighbors who know you are working at home think nothing of dropping by unannounced for coffee.

In 1961, shortly after *To Kill A Mockingbird* was published, Harper Lee told interviewers that her second novel was already begun. Its subject, she said, would be the eccentric characters who seemed to abound in small southern towns.

More than twenty years have gone by since Lee gave this description of her forthcoming work, and the novel has yet to appear. Nor has Lee ever given a public explanation for the long delay.

The success of *To Kill A Mockingbird* was by no means a fluke. The novel was the product of a long dedication to the craft of writing, and years of hard work devoted to shaping the manuscript into its final form. Perhaps the best measure of the novel's quality is that it has aged very little in two and a half decades. Readers still see themselves in the characters of Scout and Jem Finch, and are moved in turn to tears and laughter by the story.

THE NOVEL

The Plot

The story begins during the summer when Jean Louise Finch, nicknamed Scout, is six years old, and her brother Jem is about to enter the fifth grade. One day the two children meet a new playmate, seven-year-old Dill, who has come from Mississippi to spend the summer with his Aunt Rachel. Dill is fascinated by the neighborhood gossip about "Boo" Radley, a man in his thirties who has not been seen outside of his home in years. Egged on by Dill, Jem and Scout try to think up ways to lure Boo Radley out of his house, and they play games based on various stories they have heard about the Radley family. Their favorite part of the game is acting out an incident in which Boo Radley supposedly stabbed his father in the leg with a pair of scissors.

When fall comes, Scout enters the first grade. Because she has already taught herself how to read and write, Scout finds school a disappointment. Both she and Jem are intrigued, however, by the discovery that someone has been leaving small gifts in a knot-hole in one of the large oak trees on the corner of the Radley property.

Soon it is summer again, and Dill returns for another visit. The children's schemes for making contact with Boo Radley grow bolder this year, and on Dill's last night in town they decide to sneak up onto the Radley porch and spy on Boo through the window. Jem goes first, but just as he reaches the window, Nathan Radley, Boo's brother, catches sight of the children and frightens them off with a blast from his shotgun. Jem is in such a hurry to get away that he leaves his trousers behind when they catch on a wire fence. That night Jem goes back to retrieve his pants and finds that someone has mended them and left them neatly folded over the fence, as if just waiting for his return.

By now Jem realizes that Boo Radley is not a monster after all, but has been playing along with the children's games. Scout does not figure this out until the following winter, on the night that the house of their neighbor, Miss Maudie, burns to the ground. While Scout is standing outside in the cold watching the fire, someone sneaks up behind her and places a blanket around her shoulders. Later, Scout and Jem realize that there was only one person in town who was not already at work fighting the fire—Boo Radley.

Now that Jem and Scout realize that Boo Radley is basically a kind person, their interest in the Radley family begins to fade. In the meantime, however, they learn that their father Atticus has become the defense lawyer for Tom Robinson, a black man who is charged with raping Mayella Ewell, a white girl. At first the children care about the case only because it means that their friends have begun to call Atticus nasty names. Atticus warns them that they mustn't get drawn into fist fights over these taunts.

Scout manages to keep out of fights until Christmas day, when her least favorite cousin calls Atticus a "nigger-lover," and she responds by punching him. After this incident Scout and Jem begin to think that perhaps their father's hatred of violence is just a sign of weakness on his part. Their suspicions are supported by Atticus' dislike of hunting. Although both children have received air rifles for Christmas, their father makes no secret of his disapproval. Then one day a mad dog wanders into the neighborhood and the sheriff calls on Atticus to put the animal out of its misery. The children learn for the first time that their "feeble" father was once the best marksman in Maycomb County, and has given up shooting out of choice, not fear.

Even knowing this, the children find it hard to follow Atticus' example and hold their tempers. One old lady in the neighborhood, Mrs. Dubose, makes Jem so angry with her insulting remarks about Atticus that he destroys every flower in her garden. To make amends Jem has to read to Mrs. Dubose every afternoon for two months. Only after Mrs. Dubose has died do Jem and Scout learn that the old lady was struggling to overcome an addiction to drugs. Atticus tells the children that Mrs. Dubose, unpleasant as she may have been, was a truly brave woman. Courage, he says, is not "a man with a gun," it is the willingness to fight back even when the odds are stacked against you.

As the trial of Tom Robinson grows nearer, the children become more aware of the strong feelings it has aroused in everyone in Maycomb. One day their housekeeper, Calpurnia, takes Jem and Scout to visit her church, and the children realize for the first time that the black parishioners are supporting Tom Robinson's wife because no one in town will hire her.

Two nights before the trial it to start, a group of men come to the Finch house to tell Atticus about threats against Tom Robinson's life. Atticus spends the next night camped out at the jail to defend Tom against the mob. Jem, Scout, and their friend Dill go downtown to check on Atticus and, by chance, arrive at the same time as a group of very angry men, who have come to kidnap Tom Robinson and kill him. Scout recognizes one of the men in the group as Walter Cunningham, the father of a boy in her class at school, and her friendliness embarrasses the man so much that he changes his mind and talks the mob into leaving.

The next day, at the trial, Atticus' questions make it clear that Mayella Ewell and her father are lying about the rape: Tom Robinson is innocent. Nevertheless, the jury members convict him because their prejudices prevent them from taking a black man's word against two whites. Atticus is now a hero to the black community of Maycomb, but Bob Ewell, Mayella's father, vows to "get" Atticus for showing him up as a liar in front of the whole town.

Tom Robinson, meanwhile, has given up any hope of getting justice from the courts. He makes a desperate attempt to escape from the prison exercise yard, and is shot dead. Jem and Dill, already bitter over the outcome of the trial, happen to be with Atticus when he tells Tom's wife of the death, and they are deeply affected by her grief.

By the time Halloween comes around, the Finch family has begun to put the tragedy of Tom Robinson's fate behind them. There is a Halloween pageant planned and Scout, much to her dismay, has been cast in the role of one of Maycomb's most important agricultural products—a ham. After the pageant Scout decides to walk home still dressed in her bulky costume, with Jem leading the way. The cowardly Bob Ewell, seeing an opportunity to get revenge on Atticus through his children, follows the children down a dark street and tries to kill them. In the confusion that follows Scout realizes that another adult has appeared and is fighting on their side. It is none other than Boo Radley, who had seen the attack from his window. Boo stabs Bob Ewell to death, and carries the wounded Jem home.

The sheriff decides to file a report saying that Bob Ewell fell on his own knife and died, thus sparing Boo Radley the publicity that would be sure to follow if his part in saving the children became known.

Scout never sees Boo Radley again after that night, but she has learned that he was a good man all along—not the frightening man that she and the other children imagined him to be. She has learned a lesson about understanding and tolerance. And through the sheriff's action she sees that sometimes there can be justice and compassion in the world.

The Characters

Scout

Jean Louise Finch, whose nickname is Scout, is only five-and-a-half years old when the novel begins, but she is already a complex and interesting personality. Scout's mother died when she was two and her father is a scholarly man in his fifties who has no idea of how to play with his children or talk to them on their own level. Scout has taught herself to read at an early age, and she has a vocabulary equal to that of many adults. Her habit of speaking her mind in the presence of grownups makes Scout often seem older than her years. In recalling her first day in the first grade, Scout thinks of herself and her schoolmates as little adults, who must take care of the confused first-year teachers. Later, when she is unjustly punished for getting into a fight with a cousin, Scout takes it upon herself to explain to her uncle why his methods of handling children are wrong. After these incidents we are only mildly surprised when Scout is able to find the right words to turn away a lynch mob that has come to kill Tom Robinson.

Scout is also something of an outsider. A tomboy, she is still not completely accepted by her brother Jem and their friend Dill. We never hear of her having any close friends her own age, either boys or girls. And in contrast to Jem, who is constantly disappointed by the shortcomings of human nature, Scout seems to take bad news in stride. At one point, following the conviction of Tom Robinson, Atticus Finch expresses surprise that Jem, rather than Scout, seems most likely to become embittered over the injustice they have witnessed. Perhaps you will not be surprised. Scout's sense of humor and detachment seem to protect her from the disillusionments that her more vulnerable brother falls prey to.

Most readers find that the portrayal of Scout is not only interesting but highly believable. Perhaps this is because we all recall times from our own childhood when we were smarter and more aware than adults gave us credit for being. Scout is able to put this awareness into words. Furthermore, Scout's sense of humor—and her unwitting mistakes and misunderstandings—save her from being a smart aleck. We don't feel that Scout is setting herself above the adults she criticizes.

There are always a few readers, however, who conclude that the portrayal of Scout is less than convincing. They argue that many of Scout's opinions sound too adult and that she is always too ready to come up with the right words for the occasion.

Before you make up your mind about Scout, you should remember that the voice we hear narrating the story is actually that of the grown-up Scout—Jean Louise Finch—looking back on events that happened years earlier. Some of the opinions and ideas expressed in the novel are really those of the older Jean Louise. You should judge Scout by her actions and quoted words in the story, keeping these separate from the opinions of the narrator.

Atticus Finch

Atticus Finch sets a standard of morality that no other character in the book comes close to matching. Atticus is a studious man whose behavior is governed by reason. Once he decides that a given course of action is right, he perseveres regardless of threats or criticisms.

But Atticus is not a crusader. He does not go looking for causes to champion. The Tom Robinson case was not one he volunteered to handle—the judge assigned him the case because he felt Atticus would do his best to win. Atticus' desire to avoid conflict when possible is another quality that the author obviously wants us to admire. Readers may have differing opinions about this quality.

NOTE: You may have noticed that some characters' names in this story have hidden meanings. For example, Scout is a seeker, scouting out new areas of experience. Atticus' name is a reference to the district (Attica) of ancient Greece in which Athens was located. In some ways Atticus' rational approach to life is similar to that of ancient philosophers. You might look up the views of the Stoics; their philosophy has a certain resemblance to Atticus' type of southern gentleman.

Jem

Scout's older brother Jeremy, or Jem, Finch changes considerably over the course of the novel. At first you see him as Scout's playmate and equal. Once the children start school, however, Jem becomes more aware of the difference in age between himself and his sister. He doesn't want her to embarrass him in front of his fifth-grade friends. And later he and Dill develop a friendship from which Scout is partly excluded because she is a girl. In this part of the story you see Jem as the wiser older brother. He is the first to figure out that Boo Radley has been trying to communicate with them, and he does his best to explain unfamiliar words to Scout, even though he often gets their meanings wrong.

Jem is also the more thoughtful and introverted of the Finch children. Unlike Scout, who is a fighter by temperament, Jem seems determined to obey his father's request to avoid fighting. He lets his anger build inside, until one day in a fit of temper he destroys Mrs. Dubose's garden. Later, at the time of the trial, Jem's optimistic view of human nature becomes apparent. He is probably the only person in town who really believes that justice will be done and Tom Robinson found innocent. When this does not happen, his disillusionment is so great that for a time he can't stand even to talk about the incident.

By the end of the story Jem is almost grownup. On the surface, he seems quicker than Scout to put the trial behind, but inwardly, he has been more disturbed than Scout by the events of the trial. Some readers think that Jem's broken arm at the end of the story is a sign that he will be wounded forever by what he has observed. Scout, on the other hand, has been protected from harm by the hard shell of her silly ham costume—a symbol, perhaps, of the sense of humor that insulates her from bitterness.

Calpurnia

Calpurnia is the black cook and housekeeper for the Finches. She is treated almost as if she were a member of the family. In some ways she even takes the place of Scout and Jem's dead mother. But you soon learn that Calpurnia is not accepted by everyone. Some of the Finches' white friends look down on Calpurnia as a servant and are shocked to hear Atticus speak freely in her presence. At the same time, some members of

Calpurnia's black church are very critical of her being on such friendly terms with her white employer. Calpurnia lives a divided life. You learn, for example, that she learned to read and write from old law books. In the Finchs' house she speaks the very correct English of an educated person; at church, however, she converses in her friends' dialect so they will not feel she is trying to act superior to them.

Some authors might have presented Calpurnia as a sad figure. They might have been critical of her for compromising with the white society that discriminates against blacks. Most readers do not find this attitude in *To Kill A Mockingbird*, however. Lee treats Calpurnia as admirable because she has made the best of her opportunities and has not allowed herself to become bitter. Calpurnia has a sense of self-worth that is not affected by the opinions of people around her. This is a way in which she resembles Atticus.

Dill

Charles Baker Harris, known as Dill, is Jem and Scout's first friend from outside Maycomb. In many respects Dill is a contrast to Jem and Scout. They come from an old family, and have a father who loves them very much. Dill, on the other hand, is an unwanted child. He has no father, and his mother does not want to be bothered with him.

Dill has white-blond hair and blue eyes, a combination that makes him look rather like a wizened old man. "I'm little but I'm old," Dill tells Jem and Scout at their first meeting, and in some ways this is true. In his short life Dill has seen and done many things that Jem and Scout have not; he has even seen the movie *Dracula*. On the other hand, Dill's stories are not always true; some are a product of his lively imagination. Dill's imagination is the spark that sets the children dreaming of ways to lure the hermit Boo Radley out of his house. In this sense Dill is responsible for setting the action of the plot into motion.

Arthur Radley

Even though you do not see Arthur Radley, called Boo Radley by the children, until the final chapters of the book, he is important throughout the story. You know very little for certain about Boo's life. The one reliable story you are told is that he was a normal teenager who then made friends with a wild crowd. When he got into a minor scrape and was threatened with being sent away to a state school, Arthur's father promised that he would keep him out of trouble from then on. Mr. Radley kept his word all too well, and from that day Boo was never seen outside the house. And when Mr. Radley died, Boo's elder brother Nathan moved into the house and continued to rule Boo with an iron hand.

Aside from this brief family history, you don't learn much about Boo Radley. In fact, the theories that various people in the neighborhood put forth to explain Boo tell you more about the theorizers than about Boo himself. Miss Crawford, who loves gossip, spreads the tale that Boo Radley roams the neighborhood at night peeping into people's windows—especially hers. Scout and Jem, early on in the story, imagine Boo as over six feet tall and horrendously ugly, a monster who strangles cats with his bare hands and then eats them. Miss Maudie, an optimistic woman who believes in enjoying nature and the good things in life, is sure that Boo is the victim of his father's overstrict and gloomy moral code.

One story about Boo that you hear early in the novel is the rumor that he once stabbed his father in the leg with a pair of scissors. At first this sounds like nothing more than another of the children's wild ideas. Yet, late in the novel Boo stabs Bob Ewell to death. So it turns out that Boo is capable of violence after all.

Oddly enough, even as you learn that Boo actually is the killer of Bob Ewell, he seems less frightening now than he did before. Face to face with the neighborhood hermit for the first time, Scout sees that he is really a shy, pale, harmless man—a middle-aged child. You are meant to see that Boo struck out against Bob Ewell in the innocent unthinking way that a child might strike out against an act of cruelty. Thus, by the final scene of the novel the roles of Boo and Scout are reversed—he is the childlike innocent and Scout, though still a child in years, is already playing the part of the adult, protecting Boo from a world too complex for him to understand.

Other Elements

SETTING

To Kill A Mockingbird is set in Maycomb County, an imaginary district in southern Alabama. The time is the early 1930s, the years of the Great Depression when poverty and unemployment were widespread in the United States. For parts of the deep South like Maycomb County, the Depression meant only that the bad times that had been going on for decades got a little bit worse. These rural areas had long been poor and undeveloped. Black people worked for low wages in the fields. White farmers were more likely to own land, but they were cash poor. It was common for children to go to school barefoot, and to suffer from ringworm and other diseases. Although automobiles had been around for some years, most farm families still depended on horses for transportation and to plow their fields.

Scout's family, the Finches, belong to the elite of local society. Atticus Finch is an educated man who goes to work in a clean shirt. The family owns a nice house and can afford to hire a black housekeeper. Still, the Finches are well-off only in comparison with the farm families who live in the same county. They, too, have little money.

Instead of bringing people together, the shared experience of poverty seemed to contribute to making the South more class-conscious than other parts of the country. One reason why people like Scout's Aunt Alexandra place so much importance on family background and "gentle breeding" is that these concepts were just about all that could be counted on to separate a family like the Finches from the truly poor. The advantages of education, a professional career, and owning one's own home did not last long if a family happened to have a run of bad luck. The fear that the family's position could only get worse, never better, helped to turn some people into social snobs.

You will notice that none of the characters in this story takes much interest in the world beyond Maycomb County. When Scout's class studies current events in school, most of the children are not even sure what a "current event" is. Even the adults seem to take little interest in such developments as the presidency of Franklin D. Roosevelt or the rise of Adolf Hitler in Germany. People seldom travel far from their homes. And they almost never eat a meal in a restaurant, even a cheap restaurant. When Dill eats in a diner, this is enough to make him a minor celebrity in Scout's eyes.

Of course, the most important difference between the South of the 1930s and the South today is that in the 1930s a system of segregation was in force. Blacks and whites were forbidden by law to mix in schools, in movie theaters, or on trains. They could not use the same rest rooms or drink from the same water fountains. Blacks had very little, opportunity to get an education. Many kinds of jobs were not open to them. Black people were not allowed to vote. Nor could they serve on juries, not even when the defendant was a black man. Any black person (and, for that matter, any white) who challenged the system of segregation publicly would have been in serious danger of being killed by prosegregation fanatics. In fact, segregation was taken so much for granted that it is not even described in the novel in so many words. Not even Atticus Finch, the character who represents idealism and a devotion to justice, ever attacks the basic system of segregation. Nevertheless, just because Atticus believes a black man's word over a white man and woman's, many people in Maycomb feel that he is undermining the system that keeps whites on top of the social order.

By the time *To Kill A Mockingbird* was published in 1960 segregated school had been ruled unconstitutional by the U.S. Supreme Court and the struggle for civil rights in the South was underway. At this time, the South had a very bad reputation in the eyes of the world. White people in other parts of the United States tended to feel superior to the bigots of the deep South. In many cases, they had not yet been forced to confront the fact that racial prejudice existed all over the country, even though elsewhere it took less obvious forms.

THEMES

1. Prejudice

The title of the book, *To Kill A Mockingbird*, is a key to some themes of the novel. The title is first explained in Chapter 10, at the time that Scout and Jem Finch have just received air rifles for Christmas. Atticus tells his children that it is a sin to shoot a mockingbird. Later Miss Maudie explains to the children what Atticus meant: Mockingbirds are harmless creatures who do nothing but sing for our enjoyment. Therefore, it is very wrong to harm them.

It is easy to see that the "mockingbird" in this story is Tom Robinson—a harmless man who becomes a victim of racial prejudice. Like the mockingbird, Tom has never done wrong to anyone. Even the jurors who sentence him to death have nothing personal against him. They find him guilty mostly because they feel that to take the word of a black man over two whites would threaten the system they live under, the system of segregation. Tom himself is guilty of nothing but being in the wrong place at the wrong time.

It is possible that the mockingbird of the title has more than one meaning. Today mockingbirds live in many northern states, but only a few decades ago mockingbirds lived principally in the southeastern United States. Like the mint julep or the song "Dixie," the mockingbird symbolized the southern way of life—a culture that emphasized good manners, family background, and a relaxed, unhurried pace of living. Unfortunately, another aspect of this way of life was racial segregation, a system that had been tolerated for decades by many southerners who knew in their hearts that it was morally wrong.

By the time this novel was written perceptive southerners could see that the opportunity for them to take the lead in ending segregation was already past. The civil rights movement, led by blacks and supported by whites in other parts of the country, was not only ending segregation, it was transforming the politics and class structure that southerners had taken for granted for decades.

To Kill a Mockingbird contains criticism of the prejudice and moral laziness that allowed Southern society to have a double standard of justice. The novel also presents a somewhat optimistic view of white Southerners that was somewhat unusual at the time the novel appeared. The story indicates there are good human beings like Atticus Finch everywhere, even in the midst of a corrupt society. Even those who do wrong, the novel goes on to suggest, often act out of ignorance and weakness rather than a deliberate impulse to hurt others.

There are always a few readers who feel that the novel offers an overly optimistic and simplified view of human nature. On the other hand, the hopeful note it strikes may be one of the reasons for the book's great popularity. The author does not ignore the existence of evil in society, but she does suggest that human beings are born with a desire to do the right thing.

Although most readers think of *To Kill A Mockingbird* as a novel about racial prejudice, you will notice that the mockingbird theme does not apply only to victims of this form of discrimination. Boo Radley, the eccentric recluse, is another "harmless creature" who becomes a victim of cruelty. Here again, the author seems to be emphasizing the universality of human nature. Tom Robinson's problems may be bound up with the complex social problem of racial prejudice, but any neighborhood can have its Boo Radley, all but forgotten except as the subject of gossip and rumor.

2. End of Innocence

Another theme of the novel is the transition from innocence to experience. At the beginning of the story Scout's world is limited to the boundaries of her immediate neighborhood. She feels safe and secure, and totally confident that the way things are done in her home is not just the right way, but the *only* way. The arrival of Dill, who comes from a broken home and has lived in another state, gives Scout her first hint of a variety of experiences beyond her narrow horizons. Then, on her first day of school, she begins to discover that not everyone agrees that the way things are done in Maycomb, Alabama, is necessarily correct. She also learns that sometimes it is necessary to compromise in order to get along. Even though Scout's teacher's ideas about how to teach reading may be wrong, Scout must respect the teacher's authority. Her own father advises her to ignore the teacher's ban on reading at home, but to pretend to go along with the teacher's methods while in the class-room. This kind of social hypocrisy is new to Scout, and she is surprised to hear her very moral father advocating it.

As the story progresses, Scout encounters many more examples of the complexity of human motiva-tion. Sometimes characters who do evil things, such as Mayella Ewell, are nevertheless more pitiful than hateful. On the other hand, it is possible for some individuals to do the right thing for quite unexpected reasons. Mr. Underwood does not like blacks and is a mean-spirited person in general, yet he alone helps Atticus during his vigil at the jail.

By the final chapters of the novel, Scout has learned that good and justice do not necessarily triumph every time. Harmless individuals such as Tom Robin-son and Boo Radley can become victims through no fault of their own. And sometimes "the system" can do nothing to defend them. In one of the final scenes of the story, the sheriff puts compassion ahead of the letter of the law so that Boo Radley will not have to face the ordeal of publicly proving his innocence. This ending is hopeful because of the compassion shown by the sheriff but it is also troubling by suggesting there sometimes may be a conflict between the spirit of justice and the letter of the law.

3. Justice as a Simple Concept

Related to the theme of innocence and experience is the novel's suggestion that innocent children can often see large moral issues more clearly than adults. Scout, Jem, and Dill never waver in their horror at the injustice done to Tom Robinson. The adults in the story, however, see all the complexities of the situa-tion to the point of being blinded to the central issue of right and wrong. However much Scout may grow through her exposure to new experiences, one hopes that she will never lose her childlike undertaking of justice. In the view of this novel's author, justice is a simple concept. To recognize the difference between justice and injustice does not take any special degree of wisdom or sophistication. In fact, the learned members of the community—such as the judge and prosecutor—and the proudly religious Baptists who are spectators at the trial are, willingly or not, allied with the machinery of injustice.

This way of looking at justice may seem obvious, but many writers and readers do not necessarily agree with it. Some readers feel that Lee in effect stacked the deck in favor of simplicity by making Tom Robinson such a straightforward, harmless character. What if Tom had been outspoken and troublesome? What if the children had some reason, however slight, to dislike him? For that matter, aren't Scout and Jem's attitudes just reflections of the beliefs of their father? Innocent or not, the children might take a completely different view of both the trial and Boo Radley's plight if they came from a less fair and tolerant home.

If you read closely, you will see that Harper Lee does not ignore these questions completely. She has many positive things to say about the value of education and children's ability to learn morality from the examples set by various adults, including Atticus, Miss Maudie, and Mrs. Dubose. Nevertheless, the conclusion of the novel still supports the belief that justice is easy to recognize and define. In deciding how to deal with Boo Radley, the sheriff trusts his own compassionate impulse more than he trusts the law and police procedure. And Atticus, the lawyer, agrees.

You might be interested to compare the view of justice in this story with a novel that takes a very different point of view such as William Golding's *Lord of the Flies*. In Golding's novel, a group of children cast away on an island are seen as amoral creatures who become more cruel and power hungry as their memories of civilized life grow dimmer.

STYLE

Critics and reviewers of *To Kill A Mockingbird* agree that the novel is written in a straightforward, unaffected style. They do not always agree, however, on whether this is one of the book's strengths or one of its weaknesses.

A few of the novel's detractors have argued that the past-tense narrative avoids getting inside Scout Finch's six-year-old mind. We have no sense of her as a character who speaks and thinks within the limits of a childish vocabulary. In the same vein, some readers have complained that the adult characters in the story are two-dimensional and that the language of the novel lacks the depth and variety we might expect from a first-rate work of fiction.

Other readers have argued that easy-to-read prose does not necessarily lack art. The unadorned style in fact works well in communicating the world of six-year-old Scout.

One aspect of the author's straightforward approach to style is her treatment of the character's Southern accents. You will notice that in some cases the author changes spelling or runs words together to indicate the sound patterns of Southern speech. For example, characters say "Nome" instead of "No, Ma'am." Comparatively speaking, however, Lee does not go very far in this direction. Many other authors, faced with representing the speech of characters who do not use orthodox English play with spelling and word order in an attempt to represent exactly the characters' speech patterns. Lee uses Southern pronunciations just often enough to remind us of her characters' speech patterns, but not often enough to make us continually conscious of them. Some readers may suspect the author of laziness on this account. But many would say that she accomplished exactly what she set out to do: There had been a tendency for decades in the United States to portray the South almost as if it were a foreign country, set apart from the rest of America. Novelists either opted for the romantic and totally unrealistic antebellum image of gracious plantations and happy, simple-minded slaves—or they went to the opposite extreme, portraying Southern whites as peculiar, backward, and, often, degenerate. In choosing a straightforward, literate style Lee minimizes the "differentness" of her characters. Good or bad, right or wrong, they are people we can imagine encountering in towns throughout the United States.

POINT OF VIEW

Scout Finch is not only the most important character in the novel, she is also the narrator. Everything that happens is seen through her eyes.

The author's decision to use a child to tell the story is a very important element in *To Kill A Mockingbird*. Scout had no comprehension of the complex web of sexual fears and racial prejudice that made so many white Southerners recoil in horror at the very idea of sexual contact between a white woman and a black man. It is not even clear that Scout ever understands what rape is, even though she claims to understand.

In choosing to present the events of Tom Robinson's trial through Scout's eyes the author seems to be saying that all the analysis that might be spent exploring the roots of racism and sexual fears and insecurity would be a waste of time. None of these things are the main issue. The main issue is one of simple justice. Scout, in her innocence, sees this.

Even so, the child narrator might not be satisfactory were it not for the fact that Scout is a rather unusual child. She has her share of definite opinions and is not afraid to pass judgment on adult affairs. If Scout were a more usual child we might doubt that she is capable of understanding what is going on all around her.

Any author who sets out to write a first person story—one in which the narrator speaks of his or herself as "I"—has certain problems to face. Everything that happens in the novel must be known to this one character, the narrator. We can never see "inside the heads" of the other actors in the story. If *To Kill A Mockingbird* had been told in the third person—by an all-knowing narrator—or in the first person, but from the points of view of a number of different characters, it would be a different novel. We would probably be told why Atticus took Tom's case and what doubts and fears he may have had as the trial progressed. We would find out what Tom Robinson was thinking during his trial and why he tried to escape. There probably would also be much more explanation of how Tom's frame-up could come about.

Some readers feel that unless the author is very clever, first person stories tend to be too limited. Others like these novels because they can put themselves in the place of the "I" of the story and become very involved. You will have to make up your mind which group of readers you belong to.

STRUCTURE

Harper Lee originally set out to write a collection of short stories, and there are readers who feel that the finished form of *To Kill A Mockingbird* remains a collection of episodes loosely strung together. Other readers admire the way the author has woven the tales of Boo Radley and Tom Robinson, so that strands of the plot complement other strands.

It is true that some chapters and parts of chapters could be lifted out of the pages of the book and read as stories in their own right—for example, the story of Atticus and the mad dog, or the chapter dealing with the death of Mrs. Dubose. (This can also be done with many other novels.)

On the other hand, if you read carefully, you will see that the structure of the novel is not quite so simple as it seems at first glance. The novel is divided into two parts. In part one, Scout, Jem, and Dill are absorbed in childish games and fantasies. In part two, they begin, in the words of the Bible, to "put away childish things." You may notice that events in the early part of the novel, which at the time seemed merely amusing, foreshadow something that occurs later on. For example, Scout's meeting with the Cunningham and Ewell boys in the first grade prepares us for our later meeting with the adult members of these families.

The Story

PART ONE

CHAPTER 1

"When he was nearly thirteen, my brother Jem got his arm badly broken at the elbow."

Almost from the moment you read the first sentence of the novel you are aware that you are in the hands of a good storyteller. The narrator, Scout Finch, lets you know right away that Jem was not seriously hurt; he recovered in time to realize his dream of playing high-school football. But at the same time, Scout is in no hurry to tell you *how* her brother happened to break his arm. You will not learn the answer to this question until the final chapters of the story.

For the meantime, leaving you in suspense about the cause of Jem's broken arm, the narrator backtracks into what may at first seem to be a series of irrelevant digressions.

First of all, you learn a little bit about the history of Scout's family. The first Finch to settle in Alabama was a devout Methodist who broke only one of his church's rules—the one against owning another human being. Simon Finch was a slaveowner. After him came a series of descendants who stayed on the same piece of land, making a modest living as farmers. Scout's father Atticus and her Uncle Jack broke the family tradition by going into professions. Atticus became a lawyer, and Jack studied medicine.

NOTE: You may wonder as you read this section what this family history can possibly have to do with the plot of the novel, and the question of how Jem broke his arm. These few paragraphs have raised several subjects that become very important to the story later on—the evils of slaveowning, the importance of family tradition in the South, and Atticus' dislike of being on the losing side of a criminal case.

Scout Finch goes on to describe her hometown of Maycomb, Alabama. Maycomb, you are told, was a "tired old town" where people moved slowly and nothing ever seemed to happen. "A day was twenty-four hours long but seemed longer."

If Maycomb is a small, isolated town, Scout Finch's world is even smaller, limited to the boundaries of her immediate neighborhood. At the time the story begins, Scout is going on six years old. Her mother died when she was only two, and her father Atticus is an older man who often seems remote from his children.

One day, Scout and her older brother Jem discover that there is a new boy in the neighborhood. He is Charles Baker Harris, nicknamed Dill. Dill is spending the summer with his Aunt Rachel, and although he is not quite seven years old—just a year older than Scout, and three years younger than Jem—he has had many experiences that seem exciting to Jem and Scout. For example, he comes from a town with a movie theater, and can tell the stories of many movies.

In return, Scout and Jem entertain Dill with tales about the local mystery man, Boo Radley. Boo is a man in his thirties who is never seen outside of his house. The children know about Boo only from local gossip and legends. One story is that he once stabbed his father with a pair of scissors. And the neighborhood gossip, Miss Stephanie Crawford, claims that Boo is a peeping Tom who sneaks out of his house at night and spies in people's windows. The rest of the

Radleys are almost as strange as Boo. They seem to have no friends, and their house is always shut up tight, even in the hottest part of the summer.

NOTE: Perhaps you can remember from your own childhood a house that was rumored to be haunted, or a family that the local children believed to be odd or even scary. If the rumors were not really true, you did not want to know about it. It was fun and exciting to believe them, at least for a time. Something similar is going on with Scout, Jem, and Dill. They imagine that Boo Radley is six and a half feet tall, eats raw squirrels and cats for dinner, and has perpetually bloodstained hands. They even dare each other just to run up to the Radley house and *touch* it. The stories about Boo Radley are a source of excitement in an otherwise dull small town. On one level, perhaps, they don't really believe the tales about Boo Radley, but they try their best to pretend that they are true.

CHAPTER 2

When September comes Dill goes back to Meridian, and Scout begins to look forward to starting first grade. Jem tries to warn his sister that school and home are two completely different worlds. She will have to adjust to a new way of behaving. And above all, she mustn't embarrass him by talking about their childish games in front of his fifth-grade friends!

In spite of these warnings, Scout is full of confidence. Her teacher, Miss Caroline Fisher, is a pretty young woman in a red and white striped dress—"She looked and smelled like a peppermint drop," Scout thinks to herself. However, much to Scout's shock, Miss Caroline is not at all pleased to discover that

Scout can already read perfectly well. Miss Fisher has come prepared to install a modern system for teaching reading, and it upsets her that Scout has managed to learn to read at home, without the benefit of any system at all.

Miss Caroline is totally unable to see the humor in her preference for students with "fresh minds"—that is, empty ones—and she promises, in all seriousness, to "undo the damage" of Scout's already knowing how to read.

NOTE: Scout's confusion increases when Jem tells her at recess that Miss Caroline's system of teaching is something called the "Dewey Decimal System." Of course, Jem is wrong about this. The Dewey Decimal System, devised by Melvil Dewey, is a way of shelving books in libraries; it has nothing to do with the theories on progressive education of John Dewey, which are what Miss Fisher has in mind. This is one of many occasions in the early part of the story when Jem's explanations turn out to be amusingly inaccurate.

As the morning goes on it turns out that Miss Caroline has other problems besides her modern ideas about how to teach reading. Miss Caroline comes from the northern, less rural part of Alabama, but when it comes to understanding the ways of Maycomb County she might as well be from a foreign country. Before lunch, when she notices that a boy named Walter Cunningham has "forgotten" to bring anything to eat, she offers to lend him a quarter to buy his meal. The children are aghast. All of them know that the Cunninghams are very poor and far too proud to accept a handout from anyone. Since Walter is too tonguetied to explain why he doesn't want to take the money, it falls to Scout to explain to the teacher what the Cunninghams are like. Miss Fisher is convinced by now, that Scout is a know-it-all, and she raps her knuckles with a ruler.

NOTE: Many of you can probably remember being as confused as Scout on the first day of school. Suddenly there are a whole new set of rules to remember. And in place of your parents, who know everything about you, is a stranger who may misunderstand your attempts to be liked. Many authors would have written this scene in a way that asks you, the reader, to feel sorry for Scout and the other children. But Harper Lee makes the episode humorous. How does she do this? If you reread the chapter, you will notice that the humor comes from Scout's belief that Maycomb County, Alabama, is the center of the universe. No matter what may happen in the classroom, Scout is where she belongs, and Miss Caroline is just a misguided outsider. As Scout's opinions about Maycomb change, the mood of the story will gradually darken.

CHAPTER 3

Scout's first day at school continues. When the class is dismissed for lunch, Scout's first impulse is to beat up Walter, whom she blames for getting her in trouble with the teacher. Her brother Jem has another idea. He suggests that they invite Walter home for lunch.

You have already learned that Atticus once did some legal work for the Cunningham family. Although too poor to pay in cash, the family had paid the debt by bringing stovewood, hickory nuts, and holly to the Finches' back door. Scout thinks of the Cunninghams as poor, uncultured farm folk, and she is surprised that her father treats Walter as an honored guest. Walter has already failed first grade several times because of absences due to working on his parents' farm, and Atticus talks to the boy almost as if he were an adult. When Scout makes fun of the way Walter slathers his food with molasses—a country custom, rather like the habit of pouring ketchup over everything—it is she who is sent away from the table in disgrace. Notice that it is Calpurnia, not Atticus, who makes Scout leave the table. Calpurnia is black, and a servant, but her role is in many ways that of Scout and Jem's mother. She makes rules, establishes order, and must be obeyed just like any other adult. At the same time, it is obvious how much she and the children love one another.

Later that afternoon, back in school, Miss Caroline learns another lesson about country kids. One of the boys, Burris Ewell, has "cooties" (lice). When he is ordered to go home and bathe, Burris turns surly and threatening. This time Miss Caroline is happy to let her students take over and deal with Burris. He leaves the classroom after announcing that he had never intended to stay anyway: Ewell children attend school only on the first day of every year to keep the truant officer happy.

That evening, Scout begs Atticus to let her quit school, too. Miss Caroline has told her to stop reading at home with her father in the evenings, and Scout does not want to give up the one special pleasure she shares with Atticus. Atticus suggests a compromise: Scout can keep on reading at home, but she will have to go back to school and try to get along better with her teacher. Part of growing up, Atticus says, is learning to deal with people like Miss Fisher and Walter Cunningham, who have different ideas about how things are done.

"You never really understand a person until you consider things from his point of view—until you climb into his skin and walk around in it," Atticus tells her. This is a piece of advice that Scout will recall many more times in the course of the story. You might almost say that the entire novel is about how Scout learns to put her father's words into practice.

NOTE: By now you have heard another of Jem's mixed-up definitions. The legal problem that the Cunninghams brought to Atticus had to do with an *entailment*. Jem tells Scout that an entailment is "the condition of having your tail in a crack." Actually, an entailment is a kind of restriction on what an owner can do with his property.

CHAPTER 4

Scout's year in first grade soon settles into a boring routine. Nothing really interesting happens until the spring, when Scout and Jem discover that someone is leaving small objects in a knothole in an old oak tree on the corner of the Radley property. At first, when Scout finds two sticks of chewing gum wrapped in shiny silver foil, Jem warns her not to chew them—anything found on the Radley property might be poison! But when he finds two old Indianhead pennies in the knothole, Jem takes a different attitude. Indianhead pennies are good luck charms that he has always wanted to own.

When summer begins and Dill comes back to town the children's games become more exciting. One day they decide to take turns rolling down the street inside an old car tire they have found. On her first ride, Scout gets pushed too fast and ends up careening into the forbidden territory of the Radleys' front yard. She doesn't tell the boys, but she is sure that she heard someone laughing at them from inside the Radley house.

Dill's other idea for a game is that the three of them should act out scenes from the stories they have heard about the Radleys. The scene that the children enjoy play-acting the most concerns the rumor that Boo Radley once stabbed his father with a pair of scissors.

In this chapter it almost seems as if Atticus' advice about trying to understand other people's ways has been totally forgotten. The games of Jem, Scout, and Dill have a childish innocence, but they can be cruel. It never occurs to the children that the Radleys might not appreciate having their private problems dramatized for the whole neighborhood to hear. Also, when Jem and Dill start to talk about ghosts and superstitions, Scout dismisses their stories as "nigger talk." She has no idea that "nigger" is not a nice word, or that there is anything prejudiced about her remark.

NOTE: Were you shocked to find Scout, the heroine of the story, using the word "nigger"? Notice that the word makes its first appearance in the novel in a very casual, offhand way. The author never tells us in so many words that there is anything wrong with Scout's attitude. (In the 1930s, when the story takes place, "nigger" was a common word in the South.) But there is a hint that the subject of racial prejudice may become more important later on in the story. You know that Atticus is a good man, and that he disapproves of the children's "Radley family" game. Scout's comment about "nigger talk" has been put in the same category as the children's tormenting of the Radleys—another instance of unthinking and unintentional cruelty.

CHAPTER 5

As the summer goes on, Jem and Dill become inseparable buddies. For the first time, Scout feels left out because she is a girl. In reaction, she forms a special friendship with Miss Maudie, a widowed lady who lives next door.

Miss Maudie, you are told, hates her house and so spends as much time as possible working outdoors in her garden. A kind, gentle person, she tries to make Scout see that Boo Radley is a real human being who deserves her sympathy. Miss Maudie suggests that Boo Radley's fear of leaving the house may have something to do with his father's too strict views on religion. She compares Mr. Radley to a certain sect of Baptists who think that it is sinful to enjoy any form of beauty, even a lovely garden. And she adds that these same Baptists believe that women are a source of evil and temptation.

Miss Maudie also makes fun of Miss Stephanie Crawford, the neighborhood gossip. Miss Stephanie claims that she has caught Boo Radley peeping in her bedroom window late at night. When Miss Maudie heard this tale, she immediately asked, "what did you do, Stephanie, move over in the bed and make room for him?"

The humor in this chapter comes from the fact that Miss Maudie's remarks about sex go right over Scout's head. Scout has no idea that Miss Maudie was accusing Miss Stephanie of being sex-starved. Bewildered, she concludes that Miss Stephanie's reaction to the comment must have had something to do with Miss Maudie's loud, booming voice.

In the meantime, the author has used Miss Maudie's opinions to give you a point of view that would never occur to Scout, perhaps not even to her father,

Atticus: A lot of the unpleasantness in the world may have something to do with the belief that sexual pleasure is always sinful. When people become afraid of facing their own feelings about sex, their fear sometimes spills over into a suspicion of anything that is unfamiliar or different.

At this point in the story, you may feel that Miss Maudie's opinions come out of nowhere. You certainly haven't heard anything to connect Boo Radley's strangeness with anything having to do with sex. Later, however, you may have occasion to remember Miss Maudie's comments—when the subject of rape comes up in a context that has nothing to do with Boo Radley.

CHAPTER 6

On the last night of Dill's summer visit, he and Jem come up with their most daring game yet. They are going to sneak up onto the Radley porch after dark and peek through a window. Against her better judgment, Scout decides to go along.

Jem goes first, and he has just crawled across the porch to one of the windows when, suddenly, Scout sees the shadow of a man fall across the porch. The three children run for their lives, and as they flee a blast from a shotgun pierces the air. In their hurry to get away, Jem's trousers get caught on a wire fence. He jumps out of them and runs for his life.

The whole neighborhood knows within minutes that Nathan Radley, Boo's older brother, has taken a shot at an intruder on his back porch. Nevertheless, Jem and Dill think that they have fooled Atticus with their explanation that Jem lost his pants to Dill in a game of strip poker! To get away with this explanation, however, Jem will have to get his trousers back.

In the middle of the night, trembling with fear, Jem slips out of the house and retrieves the trousers from the Radley's fence.

CHAPTER 7

For a whole week after the shotgun incident Jem is unusually moody and quiet. Finally, he says to Scout that when he returned to the fence he found that someone—he does not know who—had mended his torn trousers and hung then neatly over the wires.

Later that fall, the children discover that once again someone is leaving small treasures in the knothole of the big oak tree. They find two small dolls carved out of soap, a whole pack of chewing gum, and finally an old pocket watch with a penknife attached. Jem suggests that they write a thank-you note to whoever is leaving the gifts for them. But before Scout and Jem can deliver the note, Nathan Radley fills the knothole with cement. When Jem asks Mr. Radley why he filled the knothole, he replies that it was because the tree was dying and the cement would stop the rot from spreading. Atticus, however, tells Jem that the tree was perfectly healthy.

NOTE:　　In this chapter you can see clearly that the disparity in age between Scout and Jem has begun to make a difference. By now, Jem obviously knows who has been leaving the small gifts in the knothole. Perhaps you figured out even before he did that it was none other than Boo Radley. Scout, on the other hand, is still so caught up in her image of Boo as a frightening man that she doesn't guess the solution to the mystery. Nor does she understand why Mr. Radley's filling up the knothole makes Jem so sad. Jem, of course, knows that Mr. Radley deliberately put an

end to his recluse brother's friendly attempt to make
contact with the children.

CHAPTER 8

That winter, for the first time in more than a hundred years, snow falls in Maycomb County.

At first, the snowfall is a great treat. Although there
is not enough snow to make a real snowman, Jem
figures out a way to make a snowman out of mud and
then cover it with a thin layer of snow.

But that same night, the unusual cold becomes the
indirect cause of a tragedy. In an attempt to keep her
house plants from freezing, Miss Maudie leaves the
flue of her kitchen stove open when she goes to bed.
Her house catches fire and burns to the ground.

While Jem and Scout are outside in the freezing cold
watching the neighbors rescue furniture from Miss
Maudie's burning house, someone sneaks up behind
Scout and places a blanket around her shoulders. In
all the excitement, Scout doesn't even realize that this
has happened until Atticus notices the blanket and
wonders where it came from. Jem is the first to figure
out that the blanket can have come only from Boo
Radley, since he was the only person in the neighborhood who wasn't helping out at the scene of the
fire.

Scout is terrified at first by the thought that Boo
Radley was actually able to sneak up behind her without her knowing it. Jem, however, explains what he
has known for some time—that Boo Radley is really a
kind, gentle person in spite of his strange ways. Jem
even convinces his father that they had better not
return the blanket, in case Nathan Radley decides to
punish his brother for giving it away.

After this chapter you won't hear any more about Boo Radley for some time. In one way the mystery surrounding Boo has been resolved. Both Jem and Scout have learned to understand that he is a real human being, with feelings just like anyone else's, not a figure of fun or a spooky villain. They have been able to follow Atticus' advice not to judge a person until you have seen things from his or her point of view.

NOTE: Are you satisfied with this resolution? You may have noticed that it never seems to occur to any of the adults in the neighborhood that perhaps they ought to do something to help Boo Radley. Even though everyone knows that Boo's brother Nathan is a mean man, and probably partly responsible for Boo's fear of going outside, no one in Maycomb would think of interfering in what they see as a family matter. This attitude is typical of the small-town mentality. There is not much privacy in a small town to begin with, and the citizens may fear that if they were ever to start meddling in other families' private affairs life would become unbearable.

As the story goes on you will see that there are times when the author is very critical of this mentality. The people of Maycomb are portrayed as cowards for sitting by and refusing to interfere with injustice simply because they are lazy or afraid of making enemies. On the other hand, there are times when the author seems to accept this way of thinking, and even to approve of it. You will have to decide for yourself whether you agree with the neighborhood's "kindness" to Boo Radley.

CHAPTER 9

One day in the schoolyard a boy named Cecil Jacobs announces that Scout Finch's daddy "defended niggers." Knowing only that Cecil obviously intended the remark as an insult, Scout fights back with her fists. When she asks Atticus later about the remark, Scout learns that Cecil was right. Atticus is defending a black man named Tom Robinson who is charged with rape.

At first, her father's involvement with the Tom Robinson case does not mean very much to Scout. She is most upset by Atticus' request that she not get into fights when the other children call Atticus names. From now on, Atticus warns, she is going to hear a lot of criticism of her father, and fighting back will only make matters worse.

Scout keeps her promise not to fight even though other kids in her class at school call her a coward. But during the family Christmas dinner at Finch's Landing, when Scout's prissy cousin Francis calls Atticus a "nigger-lover," Scout can control herself no longer. She punches Francis and calls him a "whore-lady," a term she knows is bad even though she has no idea what it means. Since Scout does not want the adults to know what Francis said, she ends up taking the blame for starting the fight and using bad language, and gets a spanking from her Uncle Jack.

Scout later tells Uncle Jack in private why she thinks the spanking was unjust, and he agrees with her that he doesn't understand children very well. It is only after this that Scout overhears a conversation between her uncle and her father that gives her some hint of just how much trouble lies ahead for the family. Atticus tells Jack that Scout and Jem "will have to absorb some ugly things pretty soon," and he hopes the experience will not leave them bitter. He also says that he hopes they will not catch "Maycomb's usual disease"—that is, bigotry.

You have seen in earlier chapters that Atticus is a wise man who tries to live by high ideals. But perhaps he has also struck you as a cold, withdrawn man who is rather remote from his children's lives. This is certainly what the rest of the Finch family thinks. Aunt Alexandra Finch, especially, accuses Atticus of letting the children run wild and encouraging Scout to turn into an incorrigible tomboy. Here you see that Atticus understands the children better than even they suspect. He purposely lets Scout overhear his conversation with Uncle Jack because he knows that what he has to say will make more of an impression if Scout thinks she is eavesdropping on a conversation that she is not supposed to hear. The trick works. It is only years later that Scout realizes that Atticus meant for her to hear his warning all along.

CHAPTER 10

In this chapter you continue to learn more about the character of Atticus.

Jem and Scout have always been bothered by the fact that Atticus is much older than the fathers of their friends. What's more, Atticus doesn't do any of the things that the other fathers seem to enjoy. He never goes hunting or fishing; he even excuses himself from playing tackle football with Jem on the grounds that he is too old for such games.

Perhaps this is why Atticus doesn't believe in fighting back with fists. Maybe he is just too old to understand. Maybe he is even a little bit of a coward. Both

Scout and Jem are too loyal to their father ever to voice their worries in quite this way, but the suspicion may well have occurred to you that Atticus does not believe in physical violence because he is too weak to have a chance of winning.

These suspicions may be reinforced by Atticus' wary attitude toward guns. Both Jem and Scout have received air rifles for Christmas, but Atticus makes it quite clear that he does not approve. The children are allowed to have air guns only because shooting is a universal pastime for youngsters in their part of the country, and Atticus does not want the children to be set apart from their friends in more ways than are necessary.

Atticus does make Jem and Scout promise him one thing: if they have to shoot at something, they may shoot at blue jays, because blue jays were widely regarded as pests. But no matter what, they must never kill a mockingbird. This would be a "sin." Miss Maudie later explains to the children what Atticus meant. "Mockingbirds don't do one thing but sing their hearts out for us," she says. They are harmless birds, innocent of any wrong, and this is why it would be unjust to shoot at them.

One day while Scout and Jem are out hunting, something happens that proves to them once and for all that their father's philosophy of nonviolence does not come from weakness. Jem spots a mad dog heading for the street where the Finches live. The dog's odd behavior shows that it has rabies, a disease that is fatal, not just to the animal but to a person bitten by it. Calpurnia orders the children indoors and alerts the neighborhood. Soon the sheriff, Heck Tate, arrives with Atticus. But when the moment comes to shoot the dog, the sheriff hands his rifle over to Atticus, with the comment that Atticus is the only marksman who could be sure to put the animal out of its misery safely with a single shot. This is the first hint the children have ever had that their father was once known as "One-Shot Finch," the best hunter in Maycomb County.

Miss Maudie later tells Jem and Scout that Atticus gave up hunting long ago because he felt that his natural talent for shooting gave him an "unfair advantage over most living things." Jem is delighted. "Atticus is a gentleman, just like me!" Jem shouts, meaning that they are both right to avoid fighting and violence.

NOTE: What do you think of this definition of a "gentleman?" In one sense it is easy to see why Atticus' behavior is admirable. He is a gentleman because he does not find it necessary to brag and show off his talents. He doesn't feel that he constantly has to prove that he is a "real man." On the other hand, you may find that there are moments in the course of the story when Atticus seems to carry his philosophy of gentlemanly restraint too far. You seldom see Atticus express strong emotions about anything, even in the privacy of his home. You learn only later that the Tom Robinson case was assigned to him by the judge. Would he have volunteered to take the case on his own? You can't be sure. The concept of the "gentleman" is the opposite of the modern idea that it is healthy to express your feelings freely and use your talents to the utmost in order to express your inner self. You can be sure that Atticus would be horrified by this worship of self-expression—and so, for that matter, would the author Harper Lee. As you read on you will have to decide for yourself whether you agree with Atticus' values, or whether you sometimes find them too severe.

CHAPTER 11

Now that Scout and Jem are old enough to walk downtown by themselves, they frequently have the occasion to pass the house of an elderly lady named Mrs. Dubose. There is no apparent mystery about Mrs. Dubose, but in some ways she is just as intimidating as Boo Radley ever was. The old lady sits on her front porch in her wheelchair and makes nasty remarks as the children pass by. One day, in addition to her usual insults, Mrs. Dubose taunts Jem and Scout for having a father who makes his living "lawing for niggers." Jem has been able to take worse than this from children his own age, but these words coming from an adult try his self-control beyond endurance. On his way back from downtown, Jem takes Scout's toy baton and slashes the buds off all of Mrs. Dubose's prize camellia bushes.

Atticus insists that Jem apologize for what he has done, and Mrs. Dubose says that to make amends Jem must come to her house and read aloud to her for two hours every afternoon for two months. Scout goes along with Jem out of loyalty, but she finds the whole experience frightening. The Dubose house is dark and gloomy. Mrs. Dubose starts every session with more nasty insults, and then gradually drops off into a sort of drooling fit. Every day, the alarm clock that signals the end of the reading session takes longer and longer to ring, and the children suspect that there will never be an end to their ordeal.

Mrs. Dubose finally tells the children that they needn't come around any more. She dies a few weeks later. Atticus now explains to Jem and Scout why Mrs. Dubose wanted someone to read to her. It seems that Mrs. Dubose was a morphine addict. Doctors had prescribed morphine for the old lady because she was in constant pain. But Mrs. Dubose hated the thought of being dependent on a drug, and she vowed to get free of the habit before she died. The children's presence helped Mrs. Dubose to get through the agony of withdrawal without being tempted to take the drug.

Atticus tells Jem that he wanted him to help Mrs. Dubose because he wanted him to see a demonstration of courage in action. Courage, says Atticus, is not "a man with a gun in his hand." Courage is "when you know you're licked before you begin but you begin anyway and see it through no matter what."

In giving Jem this definition of courage, Atticus is obviously thinking about his own situation. He knows that he has little or no chance of winning Tom Robinson's case, but he is going to try anyway because he believes Tom is innocent. Of course, some people might argue that to carry on when you know you cannot win is not courageous, but foolish and self-defeating. How can you tell the difference between a courageous act and a foolish gesture? Is the difference just a matter of how the person involved feels? Or is there some kind of dividing line that separates one from the other? In this novel you can be sure that Atticus' ideas of right and wrong reflect the beliefs of the author. But even Scout and Jem sometimes find his views difficult to accept. For example, Jem finds it hard to forgive Mrs. Dubose for the awful things she said, even though he now knows that her meanness was in part caused by her struggle against drugs.

NOTE: You may have noticed in this first part of the novel that Scout's confusion about adult morality is often reflected in her confusion about the meaning of words. For instance, in this chapter Scout asks her father to deny that he is a "nigger-lover." Atticus replies that actually the taunt is true, since he does his best to love everyone. Why, then, do other white people use the phrase as an insult? At this point in her life Scout is just old enough to understand vaguely that people's words, like their actions, sometimes have hidden meanings.

PART TWO

In the first part of the novel Scout and Jem are innocent children who are just beginning to understand the complex morality of the adult world. So far, they have seen that some people—Mr. Nathan Radley, for example—may be evil. Still, evil has never directly touched their lives. In Part Two of the story Scout and Jem are thrust into the center of a tragedy. Tom Robinson, an innocent black man, is on trial for his life, and Atticus' role as the defense lawyer puts his whole family in danger.

CHAPTER 12

One Sunday, when Atticus is out of town on business, Calpurnia suggests that Jem and Scout come to church with her. Calpurnia is obviously proud to show off her charges to the members of her church, but not everyone there is glad to see Scout and Jem. One woman, Lulu, even demands that the children be turned out of the church. The white churches in town are all segregated, Lulu reasons, so why should a black church welcome whites?

This incident, occuring right at the beginning of Part Two of the novel, is one of the few times in this story when you are given a glimpse of the way some black people feel about whites. Up until now Jem and

Scout have always treated Calpurnia as if she were a member of their family. It never occurred to them that just as some whites hate black people, there were blacks who felt hatred and bitterness toward whites. Nor had they ever stopped to think that some blacks may have looked on Calpurnia's loyalty to her white employers as a kind of betrayal.

NOTE: The scene between Calpurnia and Lulu shows that Lee understands and acknowledges the anger that many blacks felt toward the system of segregation. However, you won't find many more references to this anger in the rest of the story. *To Kill A Mockingbird* is very much a novel about the white South, and the impact of racial prejudice on white people. Some readers have argued that this is a serious shortcoming of the novel—Lee, they say, tells only half the story. These readers point out that most of the black characters in the book are idealized and not presented in depth. You do not even find out very much about Calpurnia, who is almost like a mother to Jem and Scout. You know very little about her private life, or of her opinions about the white characters in the novel.

Other readers feel that Lee made a wise decision to limit her story to the society she knew from first-hand experience. As a white Southerner, the author could not know much about how black people talk and act when whites aren't around. Perhaps this is one reason why the author chose to tell her story from the first-person point of view of Scout, a girl very much like herself.

Once Jem and Scout get inside Calpurnia's church, they are in for another shock. At the end of the service, the minister takes up a collection for Tom Robinson's wife and children. When he decides that the parishioners have not been generous enough, he locks everybody inside the church and lectures them until they come up with more money— a tactic Scout can't imagine being used in her church. When Scout wonders aloud why Helen Robinson needs charity since she is able to work, she learns that no one in town wants to hire the wife of an accused rapist. The knowledge that in the adult world people who are blameless often suffer from guilt by association is yet another disillusionment for Scout. Her straightforward, childlike concept of justice is rapidly being undermined.

CHAPTER 13

When the children and Calpurnia return from church they find that Aunt Alexandra, their father's sister, has arrived for an extended visit. Aunt Alexandra is determined to make over Scout into a proper young lady, a prospect Scout views with horror. She also talks constantly about the importance of family background and "gentle breeding." Atticus lets the children know that he thinks Aunt Alexandra's snobbish pride in her ancestors is evidence of a twisted sense of values. He even tells them that the ancestor of whom Alexandra is most proud was nothing but a "sewer-inspector" who went crazy and tried to assassinate the president.

Nevertheless, Atticus insists that the children do their best to make Aunt Alexandra feel welcome. This is in part just one more proof of Atticus' willingness to tolerate the peculiarities and faults of others. But there is another reason for his attitude. Atticus knows that Alexandra's visit is a sign that she is taking his side against those who criticize him for defending Tom

Robinson. So in this sense perhaps Aunt Alexandra's belief in the importance of family is not such a bad thing after all. Alexandra does not really understand why her brother is taking the side of a black man who is charged with being a dangerous criminal, but she will not turn her back on a relative in his time of need.

CHAPTER 14

Alexandra's family loyalty does not stop her from getting into arguments with Atticus. First of all, Aunt Alexandra wants to fire Calpurnia. Now that the children are older, she argues, they shouldn't be under the influence of a black woman. Alexandra feels sure that she herself would set a better example, especially for Scout. But this time Atticus stands his ground. He refuses to fire Calpurnia, and he talks back to Alexandra when she tries to convince him that his involvement with the Tom Robinson case will ruin the whole family. The children have never seen Atticus argue with anyone before, and Jem tells Scout that for the time being they should be careful not to add to Atticus' troubles.

This turns out to be a hard resolution to keep. One night after she has turned out the lights in her bedroom Scout steps on something warm and smooth, like hard rubber. Terrified, Scout is sure that she has a snake in her bedroom. But when Jem comes to investigate he finds Dill hiding under Scout's bed.

Earlier, Dill had written to say that his mother had remarried. He claimed to be very happy, and told Jem and Scout that he would not be spending his summers in Maycomb anymore. Now Dill admits tearfully that he has not been happy at all. His mother and stepfather were not unkind to him, but they never seemed to want him around. Dill has run away and he begs Jem and Scout to hide him so that he won't be forced to return home.

Jem doesn't hesitate a minute. As much as he hates to betray Dill, he knows that he will have to tell Atticus that Dill is in the house. With this decision Jem has entered the world of adult responsibility. He sees at once that hiding Dill would only create more problems for Atticus, and that Dill's family must be terribly worried about him. Fortunately everything works out well for Dill. Once they get over being angry with him for running away, his mother and stepfather are happy to let him spend the summer in Maycomb with his aunt.

NOTE: Dill's appearance in a chapter that is devoted mostly to the problems caused by Aunt Alexandra presents an interesting contrast. Aunt Alexandra is always harping on the importance of family background, which is the one advantage Dill does not have. Dill has never known his real father, and his mother is indifferent to him. Yet he is a loving person, full of imagination and affection. Is Dill any worse for not having "gentle breeding?" Obviously not. Yet Dill does feel the lack of a family. He would probably be happy to have an aunt like Alexandra constantly fussing over him.

CHAPTER 15

One evening after dinner a group of men, led by Sheriff Tate and the wealthy planter Link Deas, come to the door asking Atticus to step outside and talk to them. Waiting inside the darkened house, Jem and Scout are sure that a mob has come to harm their father. From snatches of conversation they know that the talk is about Tom Robinson, and they overhear Link warning Atticus that he has "everything to lose" because of his decision to defend Tom. Finally, unable to stand by any longer, Jem calls his father to come inside and answer the telephone. The men realize that this is just a ploy to get Atticus back in the house, and laugh. Atticus later reassures the children that the men were friendly.

The next morning, Sunday, Jem and Scout learn what the men had come to discuss: Tom Robinson has been moved to the town jail. When Atticus is missing from the house that night the children realize that he must have gone to stand guard at the jail in order to protect Tom from a lynch mob. Accompanied by Dill, the children go into town to make sure Atticus is all right. Just as they arrive at the jail, a group of men pull up in their cars and gather around the jail door. Scout, thinking that these are the same men who came around to talk to her father the night before, rushes to hear the conversation.

Too late, she realizes that these are not the same friendly men she saw the previous evening. Jem and Dill, who come running up after Scout, realize that they have blundered into a dangerous situation. Even Atticus is frightened by the possibility that the mob will harm his children. But Scout's immediate reaction is embarrassment; by not sizing up the situation at once she has shown herself to be nothing but a naïve child.

When one of the men grabs Jem roughly by the collar, Scout's shame changes to anger. She lashes out and kicks the man in the groin. Then recognizing one of the men in the mob, Scout starts to engage him in nervous conversation. The man is Walter Cunningham, father of the Cunningham boy in Scout's class at school. "How's your entailment gettin' along?" Scout asks, reminding Mr. Cunningham in front of everyone that Atticus has helped him with legal problems. Scout goes on to talk about young Walter, and how she and Jem once invited him to lunch when the boy had nothing to eat. The mob has come to kill Tom Robinson, and is perfectly prepared to murder Atticus as well if he stands in their way. But Scout's friendliness shames Mr. Cunningham back to his senses. He leaves the jail, convincing the other men to come with him.

Atticus later comments that the incident at the jail was a demonstration of mob psychology. People in a group, he says, will do things that are unworthy of them as individuals. By singling out Mr. Cunningham, Scout made him start acting as an individual again, not just another face in the mob. Atticus is certainly right in saying that groups can be a bad influence. Once again, however, some of you may wonder whether his faith in the basic goodness of individuals is justified.

As Atticus and the children are leaving the jail, a voice calls out to them through the darkness. It is Mr. Underwood, editor of the local newspaper. Mr. Underwood shouts that he had the mob covered all along with his shotgun. The men could not have kidnapped Tom Robinson from the jail even if they had tried.

Scout finds herself amazed by the complexity of human nature. Everyone in Maycomb knows that Mr. Underwood does not like black people. But he is devoted to the abstract concepts of justice and fair play.

CHAPTER 16

On Monday morning the trial of Tom Robinson is scheduled to begin. Atticus tells the children to stay home, but when they see the crowds heading in the direction of the court they are overcome with curiosity and sneak out of the house.

For the most part, this chapter gives you another look at the kinds of people who live in Maycomb County and a glimpse of their attitudes toward the trial. At one extreme is Scout's Aunt Alexandra, who does not even want Atticus to mention Braxton Underwood's hatred of blacks in front of Calpurnia. Alexandra believes in putting up a false front, and it makes her nervous to think that a black servant may be judging her in silence.

At the other extreme is Dolphus Raymond, a wealthy, white eccentric who has married a black woman. Mr. Raymond can get away with this only because he is rich and is rumored to be a drunkard whose judgment is clouded by whiskey.

Miss Maudie is one of the few people in town who have decided to stay away from the trial. Even Miss Maudie's nemesis the "foot-washing Baptists"—the same sect that thinks that gardening is sinful—have turned out in force. There is a carnival mood in the air, and most of the white spectators behave as though they have come out to see an entertainment.

The courtroom is so crowded that Scout, Jem, and Dill find it impossible to squeeze inside. Finally, they decide to sneak into the balcony to sit with the black spectators.

CHAPTER 17

The children have arrived in time to hear Heck Tate testify about the basic charges against Tom Robinson. Sheriff Tate was called to the house of Bob Ewell one night, where he found Bob's nineteen-year-old daughter Mayella badly beaten. Mayella accused Tom of raping her.

You may remember the Ewell family from Chapter 2 of the story. It was Burris Ewell who showed up on the first day of school with lice, and then threatened the teacher when she ordered him to go home and take a bath. The Ewell family lives near the Maycomb town dump, adjoining the black section of town. They receive public assistance, but everyone knows that Mr. Bob Ewell spends most of his relief checks on whiskey, letting his children go hungry much of the time. The Ewells are the town outcasts, and it is most unlikely that anyone would take their word against any white citizen in town. Today, however, Bob Ewell has been cast in the role of the hero. Most of the local citizens crowding the ground floor of the courtroom feel that it would be a disgrace for a black to win in a dispute with any white, so they are prepared to take Bob Ewell's side.

Bob Ewell makes the most of his temporary celebrity. He annoys the judge by making wisecracks on the witness stand and then throws the entire courtroom in an uproar by announcing in a booming voice that he actually witnessed Tom Robinson in the act of raping his daughter.

Atticus is the only calm person in the room. He has already gotten Heck Tate to testify that Mayella was bruised on the right side of her face. Now he tricks Bob Ewell into signing his name in front of everyone: Bob Ewell is left-handed.

Jem, seated in the balcony, immediately sees the significance of this piece of evidence. If a left-handed person had beaten up Mayella, that would account for the fact that she was bruised on the right side of her face. Jem is elated, thinking that his father has uncovered the proof of Tom's innocence. Scout is more realistic. She has by now figured out that it will take more than a good piece of detective work to save Tom Robinson.

CHAPTER 18

Now it is Mayella's turn to take the witness stand.

Mayella testifies that one day she was sitting on her porch when Tom Robinson happened by and she offered to pay him a nickle to break up an old piece of furniture into kindling wood. Instead, Tom followed her inside the house, grabbed her around the throat, beat her up, and raped her.

Throughout her testimony Mayella is very nervous. She seems afraid of Atticus, and thinks that when he calls her "Miss" he is trying to make fun of her. It is obvious that Mayella is not used to being treated politely.

Mayella breaks down in tears as she describes her desperate struggle with Tom. After she is finished speaking, Atticus asks Tom Robinson to stand up. Everyone present can see that his left hand is useless and mangled, the result of an accident years ago. It is difficult to imagine how Tom could have fought in the way Mayella described.

CHAPTER 19

There is only one witness for the defense: the accused man himself.

According to Tom Robinson, the incident when he broke up a piece of furniture actually took place months earlier. Since that time, he had done many small favors for Mayella. On the day the rape is supposed to have happened, Mayella asked him to come inside the house to fix a door. But once they were alone together, Mayella kissed him. Tom's reaction to this was panic. He knew that any involvement with Mayella would mean trouble. And when Bob Ewell came in and found him and Mayella together, Tom ran away as fast as he could.

It is obvious by now that Tom is telling the truth. How do we know this? Here are a few of the important reasons:

• Tom's left arm is crippled. He could not possibly have tried to choke Mayella with two hands, or beaten her on the right side of her face.

• You have learned earlier from Heck Tate that Bob Ewell never called a doctor for his daughter. There is no proof that she was ever raped at all.

• Bob Ewell and Mayella's stories contradict each other about what was going on at the moment Bob arrived. Bob says he saw the rape. Mayella says her father had to ask, "Who did this?"

• Both of the Ewells acted as if they weren't telling the truth. Bob Ewell was surly and aggressive; Mayella was frightened of Atticus because she knew he could see through her lies.

Tom Robinson's problems, however, are far from over. The prosecuting attorney gives him a very hard time. At one point, he gets Tom to tell the court the reason why he did so many favors for Mayella: He felt sorry for her. Mayella had no friends, and she spent her whole life taking care of the house while her father and brothers just sat around.

This admission will be fatal for Tom. As far as the people of Maycomb are concerned, no black man has a right to feel sorry for a white woman. Inferiors are not supposed to pity their betters.

At the end of the chapter is a conversation between Dill and Scout that contrasts their reactions to the trial. Dill, the sensitive outsider, is so upset by the way the prosecuting attorney treats Tom Robinson that he feels ill and has to leave the courthouse. Scout's feelings are more complex. As a lawyer's daughter, she realizes that the prosecuting attorney is just doing his job. Perhaps he has gone too far in the insulting way he spoke to the defendant, but basically all prosecutors ask tough questions of every defendant. Scout even feels sympathy for Mayella, who, she says, must be "the loneliest person in the world." Originally, Mayella did not mean to hurt Tom. She only wanted affection. Now, one way or another, Mayella's father has convinced her that accusing Tom is the only way to restore the family's lost pride.

NOTE: Scout's reactions show just how far she has come in accepting her father's advice to try to understand people by getting inside their skin. But understanding the motives of others does not necessarily make the world a less confusing place. If the prosecuting attorney is not entirely to blame, and Mayella is not entirely to blame, then who is responsible for what is happening to Tom Robinson? Scout does not have an answer to this question. Your first reaction may be that it is all the fault of Bob Ewell, who is obviously a liar. But remember, Bob Ewell could not have hurt Tom Robinson in the way he has if it were not for the cooperation of many other people in Maycomb.

CHAPTER 20

While Scout and Dill are sitting outside the courthouse talking about the trial, they discover that the notorious Dolphus Raymond is resting under the same oak tree. Raymond sees that Dill is in tears and offers him a drink from the bottle he is carrying in a paper bag. To the children's surprise, the bottle contains Coca-Cola. Raymond confesses that he is not really a drunkard. He only pretends to be one so that other people will leave him alone and let him live the way he wants to. If the white people of Maycomb County thought that Mr. Raymond preferred to live among blacks, they would make trouble. This way, they assume that he lives as he does because respectable people do not want him around. Scout is amazed once again at the strangeness of human nature. It has never occurred to her that anyone might pretend to be worse than he is, just to win the right to be let alone.

NOTE: As you read this scene, you might ask yourself why the author interrupts the drama of the trial to introduce a minor character who plays no part in the main plot line. Notice that at one point Mr. Raymond sympathizes with Dill for being sickened by the "hell people give other people—without even thinking." Children can see such things and be upset by them, Mr. Raymond adds, but most people as they grow older learn to ignore the ugly side of life.

Perhaps Mr. Raymond has put his finger on the real villain in the Tom Robinson affair: complacency. Too many people in Maycomb are willing to go along with an unjust system simply because that is the easy way, the way things have always been.

You may not necessarily agree with this answer. Perhaps you feel that to blame everyone allows the individuals who are most responsible to get off too easily. However, if you read closely, you will notice that this answer comes up more than once in the course of the story.

Dill and Scout go back into the courthouse just in time to hear Atticus' closing speech to the jury. Atticus emphasizes that he does not believe in complete equality: Some people may be born richer, or smarter, or with more talent than their fellow human beings. But there is one kind of equality that he does believe in very much—equality under the law. For this reason, he asks the jurors to do the right thing and find Tom Robinson innocent.

Atticus' speech expresses his deepest beliefs. But notice that it is also a very clever appeal to the consciences of the jurors. He never asks them to change their ingrained prejudices about race. All he asks is that they set their prejudices aside for a moment in favor of the democratic ideals they give lip service to. Instead of challenging the jurors directly, he appeals to the better side of their natures.

CHAPTER 21

Atticus has just finished his speech when Calpurnia appears in the courtroom with a note from Aunt Alexandra. Alexandra has noticed that the children are missing and has been searching for them all over town. At this point, Atticus realizes that Scout, Jem, and Dill have been sitting in the balcony watching the whole trial. Instead of being angry, Atticus gives the children permission to return to the courthouse after dinner to hear the jury's verdict. The children do come back, but they have a long wait ahead of them. Jem is elated by this because he knows that it means that the jurors are struggling with their consciences. He feels sure Tom Robinson will be acquitted.

But he is wrong. When the jury returns it is almost midnight. They have found Tom guilty.

As Atticus leaves the courtroom, the black specta-tors stand up out of respect. He is a hero to them, because they know that even though he lost the case he fought as hard as he could.

CHAPTER 22

In this chapter you find out how various characters in the story react to the jury's verdict.

Jem is the most upset of anyone because he had convinced himself that Tom had a chance to win. There is no doubt in Jem's mind who is responsible for Tom's fate. He blames the jurors.

Aunt Alexandra, rather surprisingly, resists the temptation to say "I told you so." She is shocked when Atticus comments that he is glad the children saw the trial because what happened to Tom Robin-son is as much a part of Maycomb "as missionary teas." Nevertheless, for Alexandra, family loyalty is still the most important value. On the day after the trial she even calls Atticus "brother," something the children have never heard her do before.

Dill has already started to look for ways to put the tragedy of the verdict out of his mind. He tells Jem and Scout that he wants to be a clown when he grows up, because "There ain't one thing in this world I can do about folks except laugh. . . ."

Miss Maudie's reaction may be the most interesting of all. She tells Jem and Scout that their father is one of those people who "do our unpleasant jobs for us." What do you think of Miss Maudie's reaction? You know that Miss Maudie is a good person. But doesn't her remark remind you of the complacency you saw in the last chapter? There are no easy answers to these questions. It is hard to imagine what Miss Maudie could have done to help Tom. Nor does it seem fair to expect everybody to be a crusader. On the other hand, Miss Maudie does seem to be acknowledging that she feels guilty to some degree for not doing more.

In the final paragraph of this chapter you learn the reaction of Bob Ewell, the one man in Maycomb whom you would expect to be pleased with the court's decision. Bob Ewell has promised that he will get revenge on Atticus if it takes "the rest of his life."

CHAPTER 23

Atticus is not unduly upset by Bob Ewell's threat. He knows that Bob is angry because even though he won the case, he was shown up as a liar in front of the whole town. But Atticus feels sure—wrongly it turns out—that Mr. Ewell won't act on his threat.

What bothers Atticus more is Jem's bitter reaction to the verdict. Atticus defends the jury system, although he does comment that perhaps it ought to be up to a judge to set the death penalty. Atticus also explains why most juries in Maycomb tend to be made up of uneducated farmers. Women did not serve on juries at all, this being the law in Alabama in 1935. Furthermore, most of the better-educated, well-off men in town avoided jury duty. They did not want to take sides in any controversy because they might make enemies. Atticus does give Scout one hopeful piece of information: The one juror who wanted to find Tom Robinson innocent was a Cunningham, a member of the same family whose men tried to lynch Tom the night before the trial. Perhaps Atticus' appeal to the consciences of the jurors did not go completely unheard.

Jem is starting to become more aware of the class differences that separate the people of Maycomb. He considers young Walter Cunningham to be basically a good person, yet Aunt Alexandra calls all the Cunninghams "trash" because of their poverty and uncultured ways. The Ewells are even lower on the social scale than the Cunninghams. And, of course, the blacks are in a different category altogether. No wonder there is so much trouble, Jem thinks, since people are constantly looking for reasons to despise each other.

Jem tells Scout that for the first time he thinks he can understand why Boo Radley never leaves his house—"it's because he *wants* to stay inside."

CHAPTER 24

It is now the middle of August and Scout is suffering through another of Aunt Alexandra's attempts to turn her into a young lady. Dressed in her pink Sunday-best dress, Scout is helping her aunt play hostess to a tea for the ladies of the missionary aid society. The ladies gush with sympathy for the plight of the poor people of Africa, but in the next breath they make unkind remarks about their own servants and criticize Atticus for trying to save Tom Robinson.

In the middle of the tea, Atticus arrives home unexpectedly. Out in the kitchen, where the guests cannot hear him, he tells Alexandra and Scout some bad news: Tom Robinson has been killed trying to escape from prison.

The ending of the chapter is a bit surprising. Alexandra is genuinely upset by the news, yet insists that she and Scout go back to entertain the guests, and carry on as if nothing had happened.

NOTE: The satire in this chapter is pretty obvious. Scout, who has no desire to be transformed into a little lady in any case, finds it easy to see through the hypocrisy and shallowness of her aunt's friends. And she reacts badly to Alexandra's insistence that they continue the tea—even though that is, after all, a variation of Atticus' philosophy of carrying on whatever the circumstances. In this case, however, the line between courage and putting up a false front is a fine one. You will have to decide for yourself whether Aunt Alexandra showed good manners, or whether the missionary society ladies might have learned something in the long run from seeing the family's reaction to Tom Robinson's fate.

CHAPTER 25

As Jem was the member of the Finch family most deeply disappointed by Tom Robinson's conviction, so he is the one most deeply affected by Tom's death. He and Dill happen to meet Atticus on the road and go with him to break the news to Tom's widow. The sight of Helen Robinson fainting dead away at the terrible news is one that Jem cannot put out of his mind. After that day, Jem goes through a period during which he cannot stand even to see Scout kill an insect.

Scout is saddened, too, but she is also objective enough to understand that the manner of Tom's death has given the white people of Maycomb an excuse to believe that their prejudices about blacks were right all along. If Tom had been patient, the gossips say, Atticus might have been able to win him his freedom on appeal. Instead, he acted impulsively and irresponsibly in trying to escape, especially since there

was no real chance of his succeeding. Scout takes
another view of Tom's act: Tom had given up on
white justice and decided to take his fate into his own
hands.

An editorial by Mr. Underwood, the newspaper
owner who came to Atticus' aid on the night of the
attempted lynching, expresses a similar view. Mr.
Underwood writes that killing a crippled man like
Tom Robinson is a sin—as bad as shooting a song-
bird.

Hearing about Mr. Underwood's editorial, you
can't help but recall Atticus' earlier warning to the
children that it is a sin to kill a mockingbird. In this
case, Tom Robinson—an innocent, physically handi-
capped man—is being compared to the mockingbird.
Scout feels sure that the newspaper editor was thinking not only of the prison guards, who shot to kill
when they might have been able to stop Tom simply
by wounding him. Scout knows that Mr. Underwood
is indicting the whole town because it never gave Tom
Robinson a chance to clear himself.

Mr. Underwood has been prepared to lose many
subscriptions to his paper in reaction to his critical editorial. The people of Maycomb ignore the rebuke,
however, telling themselves that Mr. Underwood
was just trying to write something flowery enough to
get reprinted in the big city paper.

NOTE: Here, again, the author seems to be telling you that the real sin of the white people of Maycomb is not cruelty but complacency. It would almost
be better if the townsfolk responded to the editorial
with anger. At least when people are angry, they are
likely to think and argue and take sides. They may
end up questioning their own ideas of right and
wrong. But the whites in Maycomb manage to avoid

the issue by finding some way to dismiss or belittle anyone who disagrees with them.

Perhaps you have encountered this kind of complacency in your own life. How do you deal with people who refuse to take you seriously, or even to listen to your side of the situation? Scout recognizes that Tom Robinson's escape was, in part, a gesture of protest against this indifference. But even though Tom paid with his life, the message of his protest was ignored.

CHAPTER 26

Scout's class in school is studying current events, and one of the children brings in a newspaper clipping about Adolf Hitler's persecution of the Jews of Germany. The teacher, Miss Gates, gives a lecture on the difference between a dictatorship such as Nazi Germany and the democratic system of the United States, and she goes on to tell the class how bad Hitler is, and how lucky they are to live in a democracy.

Scout is disturbed by this. At home that evening she mentions to Jem that after the trial she heard this same Miss Gates telling Stephanie Crawford that the decision against Tom Robinson was a good thing because it would teach the blacks in town their proper place. How can anyone be so hypocritical, Scout wonders aloud.

Jem is furious. He orders Scout to stop bringing up the subject of the trial and people's reactions to it. He doesn't want to think about the episode ever again, he says angrily. From now on, Jem is determined to think about himself, and to concentrate on his ambition to play football in high school.

Hurt and bewildered, Scout goes to Atticus for comfort. Her father assures her that Jem has not really put the trial out of his mind, he is just storing the memory away for a little while until he is better prepared to deal with it.

CHAPTER 27

As the autumn wears on it seems that the furor in town over the trial has begun to die down. In the meantime, Bob Ewell has given Maycomb something new to gossip about.

First of all, Bob Ewell is fired from his WPA job on account of drunkenness.

NOTE: The WPA, or Works Progress Administration, was set up in 1935, during the Depression, to give work to the unemployed. Very seldom was anyone fired. This incident is one more piece of evidence of Bob Ewell's incorrigibly bad character.

Also, Judge Taylor, who presided over the Robinson trial, scared a prowler away from his house late one night.

And last of all, Helen Robinson has been followed and threatened by Bob Ewell on the way to her new job working for the wealthy planter Link Deas.

In spite of these signs that Bob Ewell has not forgotten his grudge against everyone connected with the trial, Atticus is not unduly worried. Mr. Deas has promised that Bob Ewell will be sorry if he bothers Helen again, and Atticus assumes that Bob is too much of a coward to continue in the face of such warnings.

By the end of October, Maycomb has forgotten about Bob Ewell, and turned its attention to a Halloween fair that is to be held in the high school auditorium. In addition to games and booths, there will be a special pageant. Some of the children are going to represent the various agricultural products produced in Maycomb County, and Scout, much to her dismay, is cast in the part of a ham. Her costume is a bulky affair constructed out of chicken wire and brown cloth that makes it almost impossible for her to see or even to walk without difficutlty.

CHAPTER 28

On Halloween night Scout and Jem head for the high school and find themselves thinking about Boo Radley. It has been a long time since either of them was really scared of Boo, but the mood of Halloween calls up all their old fears and supersitions about the Radley place.

Remembering an old chant that was supposed to ward off spooks, Jem intones: "Angel bright, life-in-death; get off the road, don't suck my breath."

Moments later as they pass the great oak by the Radley property, someone leaps out of the darkness at them.

"God amighty!" Jem yells.

But it is only Cecil Jacobs, a boy from school, playing a joke on them.

After this scare, the Halloween pageant itself is disappointingly tame. Even Scout is too old to be impressed by the House of Horrors, a darkened room where the children are supposed to be scared into thinking that objects like cold liver and spaghetti are really the insides of a dead body.

Scout is so bored, in fact, that she falls asleep during the pageant and misses her cue to go onstage. When she finally wakes up and makes her entrance, the appearance of a ham onstage during the most solemn moment of the pageant strikes the audience as hilarious. Scout is so embarrassed by her mistake that she decides to hurry home in her costume rather than get dressed at the school and have to face everyone who laughed at her.

Jem and Scout are heading home down an unlighted street when they hear footsteps following behind them. At first, they think it is only Cecil Jacobs trying to scare them again. But when they reach the great oak tree, Jem sees that the person stalking them is not Cecil at all. He screams for Scout to run as fast as she can.

Unfortunately, it is impossible for Scout to move very fast in her bulky costume. As she struggles to regain her balance after almost tripping, the pursuer catches up to her and shatters the heavy wire frame of her costume with a savage blow. The next thing Scout knows, a fight is going on, and she can sense in the darkness that there are now four people struggling under the oak tree—herself, Jem, their pursuer, and someone else. Trying to get away, Scout stumbles over a man's body lying on the ground. Then, in the glow of the streetlight at the end of the lane, she sees another man carrying Jem slung over his shoulder.

The man carries Jem in the direction of the Finch house, and Scout follows as quickly as she can. Inside the house, Atticus and Aunt Alexandra have already put Jem to bed, and are calling the doctor.

Scout feels sure that Jem must be dead. He looked so limp when she saw him being carried into the house, and his arm was hanging in front of him at a strange angle. She waits in fear until Dr. Reynolds emerges from the bedroom and announces that Jem is very much alive. However, his arm is badly broken.

Scout goes to check on Jem for herself, and she and Atticus are standing by his bedside when Sheriff Heck Tate comes in to report on what he has found at the scene of the attack: Bob Ewell is lying dead under the big oak, stabbed with a kitchen knife.

CHAPTER 29

While Atticus is trying to take in this news, the sheriff asks Scout to describe exactly what happened. He inspects her battered costume, and comments that the heavy frame probably saved her life. Bob Ewell had been out to kill both Jem and Scout, his cowardly way of taking revenge on Atticus.

After hearing the story of the fight Sheriff Tate asks who the fourth person was, the man who rescued Jem and carried him back to the Finch house. At that moment, Scout realizes that the mysterious rescuer has been standing in a dark corner of the bedroom all along.

"Why there he is, Mr. Tate," Scout says, "he can tell you his name."

The man says nothing. Scout notices that his skin is pale and sallow looking, and his eyes are so washed out that they seem to have no color at all. His smile is weak and timid. All at once, Scout realizes who the stranger must be.

It is Boo Radley.

CHAPTER 30

Everyone except Jem, who has been given medicine to make him sleep, retires to the porch to discuss the night's happenings.

Atticus is sure that Jem must have stabbed Bob Ewell in self-defense. But Sheriff Tate disagrees. He tells Atticus that he intends to write in his report on the incident that Bob Ewell fell on his own knife.

Atticus protests at first. He is sure that the sheriff is trying to cover up for Jem. Then it slowly dawns on Atticus that it isn't Jem the sheriff wants to protect. Boo Radley, not Jem, stabbed Bob Ewell.

Why does the sheriff want to cover up Boo Radley's part in the fight?

There can be no doubt that the stabbing of Bob Ewell was justifiable homicide, necessary to save the lives of Jem and Scout. Even if Boo's case ever came before a court, he would certainly be found innocent. The court system might not work for a black man like Tom Robinson, but Boo has nothing to fear. It is not the law that the sheriff wants to protect Boo from, but the publicity. He wants to spare Boo the need to explain himself to the police and to others, and even the attention he would surely get from neighbors who would consider him a hero for saving the children's lives. As the sheriff notes, all the ladies in the neighborhood would no doubt be showing up at the Radley's door bringing cakes and pies—a friendly gesture that would be torture for a shy, reclusive man like Boo.

NOTE: Most readers agree that Sheriff Tate is doing the right thing. He is willing to bend the rules by writing a false report, but only in the name of compassion. Justice is served, perhaps not in the letter of the law, but in its spirit. By putting himself inside Boo's skin—just as Atticus advised the children to do earlier in the story—Sheriff Tate has seen that it would be much kinder to keep quiet about Boo's action.

A few readers, however, may have qualms about this ending to the novel. Isn't this bending of the law in accordance with one's feeling the same reasoning that allowed the jurors to find Tom Robinson guilty even though they must have known he was innocent? Remember, it's possible that some of the jurors did not actively want to harm Tom. Perhaps they only wanted to spare Mayella Ewell the shame of a verdict that would have shown they didn't believe her. Perhaps we would be better off in the long run if the law were applied equally to everyone. Once people start making exceptions, doesn't this open the door to a situation where there is one law for one's friends and "people like us" and another for everybody else?

There is no right answer to these questions. Scout and Atticus approve of Sheriff Tate's decision, and their view clearly represents the opinion of the author. However, you will have to decide for yourself whether you agree.

CHAPTER 31

Bob Ewell's attack and death has had one unexpected consequence: Scout's childhood fantasy of luring Boo Radley out of his house has been fulfilled.

Now that she actually finds herself entertaining Boo on her front porch, Scout finds it hard to fit that old nickname to the man she sees. Boo Radley, the mysterious and scary neighborhood recluse has become in her eyes plain Mr. Arthur Radley, a timid and nervous middle-aged man. It is difficult to imagine that this is the same person who stabbed Bob Ewell earlier in the evening.

Some instinct makes Scout understand that she will now have to play the part of the grownup and take care of Arthur. She takes him by the arm and lets him have one last look at Jem, now sleeping peacefully in his bed, and then leads him carefully back to his own house. Standing on the Radley porch for the first time in her life, Scout can see as she never could before how the neighborhood, and her own childish games, must have looked to Arthur Radley—how he must have watched with shy curiosity, and enjoyed seeing their amazement when they found his small gifts hidden in the knothole of the oak tree. Years later, when Bob Ewell attacked the children under that same tree, Arthur Radley must have felt a special obligation to protect them.

Returning home, Scout finds her father sitting up reading a book of Jem's called *The Gray Ghost*. Atticus refuses at first to read aloud to her. The story is a scary one, he says, and Scout has had enough scary experiences for one day. But Scout is not afraid: "nothin's real scary except in books," she tells Atticus.

What do you think Scout means by this? Perhaps she means that no one has the power to frighten you once you understand his motives and his way of seeing things. Even a person like Bob Ewell, who may attack you physically, has no real power over your mind.

That night Scout sleeps soundly, safe at home in her own bed. She never sees Mr. Arthur Radley again.

A STEP BEYOND

Tests and Answers

TESTS

Test 1

1. The novel both starts and ends with the _____ incident in which
   A. Scout is frightened by Boo Radley
   B. Jem breaks his arm
   C. Atticus displays his heroic qualities

2. Another meaningful title for this novel could _____ be
   A. *Scout Grows Up*
   B. *The South Shall Rise Again*
   C. *The Courage of Atticus Finch*

3. Atticus taught his children not to kill a _____ mockingbird because it
   A. is one of God's special creatures
   B. sings beautifully and harms no one
   C. brings good luck to those who truly listen to it

4. Harper Lee contrasts the poor Cunninghams _____ with the
   A. Ewells
   B. Radleys
   C. Robinsons

5. Atticus continually tries to make Scout _____
   A. stop daydreaming and focus on reality
   B. put herself in other people's shoes
   C. exhibit a more mature behavior

6. A unique facet of the Atticus-Scout _____ relationship is that
   A. they share a common vision of humanity
   B. he will accept criticism from her
   C. he never talks down to her

7. The kindness of Boo Radley is displayed _____ through
   I. the mending of Jem's pants
   II. the blanket around Scout's shoulders
   III. the bag of apricots in the Finch mailbox
   A. I and II only
   B. I and III only
   C. II and III only

8. One reason Lee presents Boo Radley is to _____ show that Scout
   A. can be frightened easily by the unknown
   B. has a fertile imagination
   C. can accept people who are different

9. Atticus' courage is seen when he   _____
   I. shoots the mad dog
   II. undertakes the Robinson defense
   III. faces the lynch mob
   A. I and II only
   B. II and III only
   C. I, II, and III

10. "The bravest person I ever knew" was Atticus' _____ description of
    A. Aunt Alexandra
    B. Mrs. Dubose
    C. Reverend Sykes

11. What role does humor play in *To Kill a Mockingbird?*

12. Why is the character of Dill important to the development of the novel? Why do you think the author included him?

13. The concept of courage is very important to the novel. Discuss.

14. What is the connection between the story of Boo Radley and the story of Tom Robinson?

Test 2

1. A man who will not associate with blacks but _____
   defends Atticus is
   A. B. B. Underwood
   B. Walter Cunningham
   C. Dolphus Raymond

2. The presence of Jem and Scout at the jail _____
   A. convinces Heck Tate of the need for a fair
      trial
   B. diverts the lynch mob from its purpose
   C. inadvertently endangers Atticus' life

3. An important insight into the characters of _____
   Jem and Scout is seen when they
   A. sit in the black section of the courtroom
   B. ask their father's forgiveness for their
      prejudice
   C. challenge their bigoted teacher in defense
      of Atticus

4. Part of the successful defense of Tom _____
   Robinson hinges on
      I. his abnormal left hand
      II. the perjury of the eyewitness
      III. Atticus' skillful questioning of
         Bob Ewell
   A. I and II only
   B. I and III only
   C. II and III only

5. In the eyes of some blacks, Tom's fault was _____
   that he
   A. tried to cross the color barrier
   B. showed pity for a white woman
   C. upset the black-white balance in
      Maycomb

6. A despicable technique that the prosecutor _____ employed was
    A. sarcasm about Atticus' motives
    B. repeated references to Tom as "boy"
    C. withholding evidence that would have cleared Robinson

7. The black community's appreciation of Atticus _____ was shown when it
    I. stood as he exited from the courthouse
    II. burned Ewell's house
    III. brought food to the Finch household
    A. I and II only
    B. I and III only
    C. I, II, and III

8. Atticus and Alexandra differed in their _____ definition of
    A. courage
    B. trash
    C. responsibility

9. In thirty of the thirty-one chapters, _____
    A. the mockingbird theme is repeated
    B. Scout is on the scene
    C. Harper Lee injects comic relief

10. "Equal rights for all, special privileges for _____ none" is Scout's definition of
    A. the ideal society of the twenty-first century
    B. the South's code of honor
    C. democracy

11. How does our understanding of Atticus Finch increase as the novel progresses?

12. What does *To Kill a Mockingbird* have to say about the nature of justice?

13. How does Scout's attitude toward superstition change over the course of the story? Discuss.

14. Explain the meaning of the mockingbird mentioned in the title of the novel.

ANSWERS

Test 1

1. B   **2.** A   **3.** B   **4.** A   **5.** B   **6.** C

7. A   **8.** C   **9.** C   **10.** B

11. In answering this question you might begin by taking note of the ways in which Scout's sense of humor make her more trustworthy and likable as a narrator. If it were done without humor, Scout's criticisms of adults—such as her first-grade teacher, Miss Caroline—and her explanations of the ways of Maycomb County might make her seem like a brash know-it-all. The humorous point of view also makes you more tolerant of the shortcomings and foibles of the white people of Maycomb, underlining the novelist's view that human beings do evil things out of ignorance, not because they are innately bad. You might also discuss the ways in which the humor in the early chapters of the story makes us aware of Scout's—and to an extent, Jem's—innocence. The children's confusion about words, and Scout's naïveté about sex, demonstrate their straightforward, childlike understanding of the world around them. The contrast between the humorous, light tone of the first part of the story and the serious developments in Part Two, makes the novel all the more emotionally affecting.

12. Dill is the first friend Scout and Jem have ever had who comes from outside the neighborhood. If you look back at the scene in Chapter 1 where Scout and Jem meet Dill for the first time, you will see that even the most ordinary facts about Dill strike them as exotic and unfamiliar. Scout and Jem have a long way to go in learning the lesson of tolerance. Dill, the outsider, is also the instigator of some of the most important events in Part One. It is his curiosity about Boo Radley that sparks the children's games. (Even the nickname "Dill" suggest that his presence adds spice to the children's games.) In Part Two it is Dill the outsider who is confused and sickened by the conduct of Tom Robinson's trial. Although Dill is a southerner, in a sense he may represent the way people from the North (also outsiders) viewed the white South at the time this novel takes place. Northerners were repelled by southern prejudice, as Dill is, but like Dill they could also put the subject out of their minds and forget it. You see Dill doing this when he says that he is going to grow up to be a clown and laugh at the world. Scout and Jem, who must continue to live in Maycomb, cannot afford to take this point of view.

13.   Whatever direction your answer to this question takes, you should begin by recalling the definition of courage given by Atticus in Chapter 11. Courage, says Atticus, is when "you know you're licked before you begin but you begin anyway and see it through no matter what." You might then go on to discuss how the actions of various characters in the story exemplify this definition of courage. Atticus obviously lives up to his own standard. He is a brave man. Miss Maudie also shows courage because she does not give in to self-pity when her house and garden are destroyed by fire. In some cases you may find it harder to decide whether characters have acted courageously or not. For example, was Tom Robinson's attempt to escape from the prison yard an act of courage? Certainly the odds were against him. Or was it a gesture of despair, or even a sign of weakness? What is the difference between courage and recklessness? Courage and stubbornness? Again, you might find at least a partial answer to these questions in the example of Atticus, a man who avoids openly heroic gestures, but who holds onto his values over a period of time, regardless of what others think of him.

14. At first you may feel that there is no connection between these two stories at all—except, of course, that Boo Radley's sudden appearance during the attack on Jem and Scout provides an exciting and surprising resolution to the novel. On second thought, however, you may begin to see other relationships. In the early chapters you see the children trying to think up ways to tease Boo, and lure him out of his house—not out of meanness but out of simple, child-like curiosity. If it were not for this aspect of the story, Scout would be in no position to judge the people of Maycomb for their persecution of Tom Robinson. As it is, you see that Scout herself is capable of intolerance. She does not take a position of moral superiority, since she herself has shared the small-town complacency she comes to blame for Tom's fate.

Note that the answer above is not necessarily the only correct response to this question. You may be able to think of other ways in which the two plot lines of the novel are related. Or you may even feel that the author has not done such a good job after all of tying the two threads of plot together. Whatever answer you give, just be sure you can defend it by citing specific examples from the novel.

Test 2

1. A   **2.** B   **3.** A   **4.** B   **5.** B   **6.** B

7. B   **8.** B   **9.** B   **10.** C

11.   Our knowledge of the character of Atticus is limited to what we learn from his young daughter, Scout. In the early chapters of the novel Scout thinks of her father as distant and strange, unlike the younger fathers of the other children in town. We do hear, in Chapter 1, that Atticus dislikes practicing criminal law because he hates to see his clients go to jail. This information could be interpreted two ways: Perhaps Atticus is a good, sensitive man; or perhaps he simply lacks the desire to fight tough battles. Scout herself is not sure which of these interpretations is true. At times, she suspects that her father is too old and weak to do anything worthwhile. In the scene where Atticus shoots the mad dog we learn that he is indeed capable of action when the situation calls for it. And in the story of Mrs. Dublose we learn more of Atticus's beliefs about courage. We are not surprised, then, when at the time of Tom's trial Atticus emerges as a hero, ready to fight for what is right even though he knows he has no chance of winning.

Throughout the novel, Atticus puts into action the right values that Scout can usually only feel and think about. But there are also times when Atticus holds back from a fight. He tries to be nice to his sister Alexandra for the sake of family unity, for example, and he won't allow Scout and Jem to fight even when the other children call them names. Unlike Scout, who sees right and wrong in very simple, straightforward terms, Atticus understands that there are times when it is important to be able to compromise.

12.   It is the children in the novel who always seem to have the clearest awareness of the line between justice and injustice. The adults, on the other hand, are frequently blinded by side issues. At the time of Tom Robinson's trial, almost everyone is concerned with something other than Tom's fate. The jurors do not want to go against public opinion and the accepted social system. The prosecutor is only doing his job. The Ewell's are desperately trying to salvage their self respect, even if it means hurting someone else in the process. No one, not even Bob Ewell, has anything against Tom personally—yet everyone has some excuse for doing him an injustice.

It is interesting to compare the events of the trial with the story of Boo Radley. In the latter case, it is the adults who condemn the children for unthinking cruelty in teasing Boo and making him the butt of their games. To a certain extent, the adults are right. But at least the children have enough sense to see that there is something very wrong with the way Boo Radley stays shut up inside his house day after day and year after year. Once again, the adults are so busy minding their own business and worrying about propriety that they have closed their eyes to a tragic wrong. What's more, Boo Radley, who is childlike in his own view of the world, understands that the children's interest is basically well meaning and does his best to communicate with them.

You may be able to think of still other times during the course of the novel when children or adult eccentrics seem to be wiser about justice than the supposedly responsible adults who can see so many sides to every question that they overlook the basic issue of right and wrong.

13.   In the early chapters of the novel Scout and her brother are fascinated by Dill's tales of "haints" and supernatural happenings. They are even thrilled and impressed that he has actually seen the movie version of *Dracula*. Dill's tales motivate them to make up their own superstitions about Boo Radley—and they dare each other to so much as touch the outside of the Radley house, as if to do so might bring on some terrible fate.

By the end of the novel, however, this childlike fascination with superstition has been replaced with a knowledge of the everyday evil of the adult world. In the final chapters, we learn that the grownups of Maycomb have even taken over organizing the children's Halloween celebrations. Having decided that the young people's pranks have gotten out of hand the adults organize a pageant that is dull and stupid. The magic has gone out of the holiday. But the threat of evil is more present than ever before, in the form of Bob Ewell who stalks and tries to kill Scout and Jem on their way home from the pageant.

In the final chapter of the story, Scout asks her father to read to her from Zane Grey's novel *The Gray Ghost*, a book she had always found too frightening in the past. Superstitions and scary stories have lost their power to terrorize Scout now that she has come face to face with the terrors that real life holds in store.

14. The title is first explained in Chapter 10 of the story when Atticus warns Scout and Jem that it is a sin to kill a mockingbird. Miss Maudie explains that this is because the mockingbird is a harmless creature who does nothing but entertain us with its song.

Atticus makes this warning at a time when he is already preoccupied with Tom Robinson's forthcoming trial, and it makes sense to draw a connection between the mockingbird and Tom Robinson. Tom, too, is a harmless creature. He has done nothing to bring on his own troubles, and his only fault is that he tried to be kind to Mayella Ewell.

After further thought, you may think of other ways in which the title relates to the events of the story. Isn't Boo Radley another "harmless creature?" Boo is the victim of his own father and brother, who are ashamed of him and who have apparently made him afraid to leave his own house.

You might also want to discuss the ways in which the mockingbird is a symbol of the good things about the traditional southern way of life, a way of life that is being destroyed from within by the evils of segregation and racial prejudice. In this case, it is the innocent children—Scout, Jem, and Dill—who are wounded by the unthinking cruelty of the adult community. They grow up carrying a burden of guilt and shame for a system they had no part in creating. Still other victims are the eccentrics and individualists like Dolphus Raymond, who have to give up their pride and place in the community in order to live and think as they please.

Finally, you might want to answer a question like this by considering the reasons why the author has chosen a bird to symbolize victims of injustice. Notice that in the novel the author seems to be saying that simple things are superior— the beauty of Miss Maudie's flower garden is more loved by Miss Maudie than her house; the innocent children see events more clearly than most adults; and so on. Does Harper Lee mean to say that civilization is the source of evil and cruelty in the world or only that civilization is the source of customs that prevent us from attacking evil head on? You will have to decide for yourself which meanings the mockingbird of the title stands for.

Term Paper Ideas

1. Discuss the concept of a gentleman that is presented in Chapter 11, where Atticus shoots the mad dog. How does that definition of gentlemanly behavior contrast with the philosophy of self-expression? With the "macho" concept of masculine behavior?

2. Who is responsible for Tom Robinson's death? What answers do various characters in the novel give to this question? What answer do you think best represents the author's point of view? What do you think?

3. What does the author's physical description of the town of Maycomb tell you about the people who live there? Notice especially the description of the town in Chapter 1. Doesn't the insistence that Maycomb is a lazy town where nothing ever happens make you feel that something very ominous is going to occur before long? How can this be?

4. Jem Finch is one of the most important and complex characters in the novel. How does his relationship with Scout change over the course of the story? Who do you think resembles Atticus the most—Jem or Scout?

5. Both Miss Maudie and Aunt Alexandra represent types of the southern lady. How do the two characters differ? How are they alike? What does Scout learn from each of them?

6. Describe the differences among the Finches, the Cunninghams, and the Ewells. What do you think of the novel's suggestion that individual members of the same family more often than not run true to type? In considering this question, pay attention to what the novel says about *why* this is so, noticing especially what Atticus has to say about heredity versus environment.

7.   How important is it to the novel that the narrator, Scout Finch, is a child at the time the events of the story take place?

8.   Harper Lee has said that the South is "the refuge of genuine eccentrics." What do you learn from the various eccentric characters in the novel, for example, Boo Radley and Dolphus Raymond? Can you think of any reasons why a society that is very conscious of class and family tradition might also have more than its share of eccentrics?

9.   Do you think the character of Scout is a convincing portrait of childlike behavior? Why or why not?

10.   The voice you hear telling the story of the novel is actually that of the adult Jean Louise Finch telling you about events that happened when she was a child. At what points in the novel do you become aware of this? How does this adult narrator's reflections contribute to your understanding of the people of Maycomb? How does the adult Jean Louise create suspense by hinting at certain developments yet to come in the story?

11.   Some readers have objected that the black characters in the novel are two-dimensional and thus the story presents a superficial view of the problem of racial prejudice. Do you feel that this is a valid criticism? In thinking about this question you might want to read a novel by Richard Wright, or some other black author presenting a view of life under segregation. How do the two viewpoints compare?

12.   Why does Mr. Underwood come to the aid of Atticus in defending Tom Robinson from the mob? Contrast Mr. Underwood's behavior with the decision of Heck Tate to file a false police report about Bob Ewell's death. How do the two men's ideas about justice differ?

13. What does the story have to say about the importance of tradition? In framing your discussion, notice that there are times when the narrator approves of tradition, for example, in defending old-fashioned ideas about education, and ridiculing Miss Caroline's modern ideas about how to teach reading. On the other hand, Atticus, the hero of the story, criticizes Aunt Alexandra for being too concerned with family traditions. And he himself violated these traditions when he became a lawyer instead of a farmer.

14. Some readers think that Jem's broken arm symbolizes the wound that the system of segregation inflicted on *white* southerners. What do you think of this idea? What evidence can you find in the story that the author might have intended to make the broken arm a symbol?

15. When *To Kill a Mockingbird* was first published in 1960 a number of reviewers compared the character of Scout with Frankie, the tomboy in Carson McCullers' play *The Member of the Wedding*. You might like to read *The Member of the Wedding* for yourself and discuss how the two characters are alike. Or, if you think they are very different, why you think the comparison is a bad one.

16. Discuss how Scout's attitude toward superstition changes over the course of the novel. Don't forget to talk about the final chapter in the story, where Atticus reads to Scout from the novel *The Gray Ghost*. Why doesn't Scout find such stories scary anymore?

17. Why do you think the scene in which Jem and Scout build a snowman was included in the novel? Explain.

18. Contrast the characters of Miss Maudie and the newspaper editor Mr. Underwood. How can two individuals whose values are so different both be "good" characters?

19.   What is the significance of Scout's criticisms of progressive education? If innocent children are sometimes wiser than the adults around them, as the story seems to be saying, why doesn't the narrator trust a system of teaching that depends on children's ability to learn through instinct and their own initiative?

Glossary

Ad astra per aspera Latin for to the stars through difficulties. An ironic choice as a motto for Maycomb County, a place progress has left behind.

Dewey Decimal System A system for organizing books in libraries devised by Melvil Dewey. Contrary to what Jem tells Scout, this Dewey has nothing to do with John Dewey, a theorist of progressive education.

Morphodite This is what Scout thinks she hears Miss Maudie calling the snowman. Actually, the word Miss Maudie used was probably "hermaphrodite," a person with both male and female characteristics.

Nome A contraction for "No, Ma'am." Harper Lee uses this spelling because it approximated the pronunciation of Southerners.

NRA-WE DO OUR PART The motto of the National Recovery Administration, whose programs were intended to help the nation recover from the effects of the Great Depression. NRA programs were ruled unconstitutional in 1935 by the U.S. Supreme Court— the "nine old men" Atticus refers to in explaining why the NRA is dead.

"One Man's Family" A popular radio serial of the 1930s.

Scuppernongs A sweet table grape common in the southeastern U.S.

Shinny A slang name for whiskey.

Smilax A vine with glossy leaves, often used for decoration.

Solicitor Another term for a lawyer. The "circuit solicitor" mentioned in the book is a government lawyer who travels from town to town prosecuting cases.

The Critics

When it appeared in 1960 *To Kill a Mockingbird* was a first novel by an unknown author. The great majority of such books are read by a few thousand, or only a few hundred, persons, and then drop quickly out of sight. *To Kill a Mockingbird* was a rare exception to the rule. It was widely read and received high praise at its publication, and it maintained a steady popularity into the 1980s.

To Kill a Mockingbird is still a relatively recent novel. Its place in literary history is by no means set. When you read the great classics of world literature you are following in the footsteps of numerous critics and scholars who have analyzed them and argued over their finer points. Some relatively recent books by such authors as John Steinbeck, Ernest Hemingway, and William Faulkner have been studied in detail and widely criticized. With *To Kill a Mockingbird*, the situation is quite different. Partly because its style is straightforward and needs little elucidation, and partly because it is Harper Lee's only published novel, it has not received much attention from scholars and critics.

At first you may feel that this situation puts you at a disadvantage. You will not find books in the library that tell you what to think about the book, or what it means.

This absence of critical studies can open the door for you. You may well have insights into the novel that are entirely original. You may notice aspects of the story that have not been studied or written about by anyone else. And you can make up your mind about the merits of the novel without having to defend your judgments against the opinions of generations of critics. You can approach the book from a fresh point of view.

The reviews that greeted the appearance of *To Kill a Mockingbird* generally were very favorable. Typical of the praise Lee's book received was this notice in the Chicago *Sunday Tribune*:

> "To Kill a Mockingbird" is a first novel of such rare excellence that it will no doubt make a great many readers slow down to relish the more fully its simple distinction. . . .
>
> The style is bright and straightforward; the unaffected young narrator uses adult language to render the matter she deals with, but the point of view is cunningly restricted to that of a perceptive, independent child, who doesn't always understand fully what's happening, but who conveys completely, by implication, the weight and burden of the story.
>
> There is wit, grace and skill in the telling. From the narrator on, every person in the book is every moment alive in time and place.
>
> —*Richard Sullivan, "Engrossing First Novel of Rare Excellence," Chicago* Sunday Tribune, *July 17, 1960.*

A few reviewers found fault with certain aspects of the novel but liked the book as a whole. Phoebe Low Adams, a reviewer for the *Atlantic Monthly* called the book "successful," but went on,

> It is frankly and completely impossible, being told in the first person by a six-year-old girl with the prose style of a well-educated adult.

Adams seems not to have noticed that you are told at the beginning of the story that the narrator is the grownup Scout looking back on her childhood experiences. Or perhaps Miss Adams knows this, but feels that the author herself failed to carry through with this premise. If the adult Jean Louise Finch is really telling the story, why does she never tells us how her attitudes toward her father, the Tom Robinson case, and other matters have changed over the years? Are you as bothered by this as Adams was?

Other reviewers enjoyed the substance of the novel, but found fault with the style. One such reviewer wrote the following:

> The praise that Miss Lee deserves must be qualified somewhat by noting that oftentimes the narrator's expository style has a processed, homogenized, impersonal flatness quite out of keeping with the narrator's gay, impulsive approach to life in youth. Also, some of the scenes suggest that Miss Lee is cocking at least one eye toward Hollywood. . . .
> —Frank H. Lyell, "One-Taxi Town," 1960
> The New York Times Book Review, July 10, 1960.

Mr. Lyell was certainly right about the story's being just right for a Hollywood movie, but notice that his reaction to the style is completely opposite to that of Richard Sullivan, quoted in the beginning of this section.

A third point of view on Harper Lee's style was presented in the magazine *Commonweal:*

> Both the style and the story seem simple, but no doubt it is quite an achievement to bring them to that happy condition.
> —Leo Ward in Commonweal, *December 9, 1960*

As far as the content of the novel goes, several critics have cautioned against the temptation to see *To Kill a Mockingbird* as only a "sociological" novel. One teacher writes:

> Students enjoy reading *To Kill a Mockingbird*, but my experience has been that their appreciation is meager. Over and over again their interpretations stress the race prejudice issue to the exclusion of virtually everything else. . . .
> —Edgar H. Schuster, "Discovering Theme and Structure in the Novel," English Journal, *October, 1963.*

Not everyone would agree with this point of view. For example, Leo Ward in the review quoted above compares *To Kill a Mockingbird* with John Steinbeck's *The Grapes of Wrath*—a novel admired in large measure for its powerful portrait of the plight of the poor and oppressed.

On the other hand, critics who tend to agree with Schuster that the novel is not so much about racial prejudice as about the universal experiences of growing up, have compared the novel with Carson McCullers' *The Member of the Wedding* and with Mark Twain's *Tom Sawyer* and *Huckleberry Finn*.

Finally, in making up your mind about the novel's ultimate literary worth, keep in mind these comments from a British review. The reviewer agrees with those who think that *To Kill a Mockingbird* is mainly a story about growing up, not a "social problem" novel. On the other hand, he agrees with Leo Ward that sometimes readers do not appreciate the art that goes into creating a novel that seems simple and straightforward:

> The innocent childhood game that tumbles into something adult and serious is a fairly common theme in fiction, but I have not for some years seen the idea used so forcefully. . . . Pretty soon we are in the adult game, based on the same fear and fascination of the dark: the ugliness and violence of a Negro's trial for rape and the town's opposition to the children's father for defending him. Miss Lee does well what so many American writers do appallingly: she paints a true and lively picture of life in an American small town. And she gives freshness to a stock situation.
> —*Keith Waterhouse in*
> The New Statesman, *October 15, 1960*